ARKA

THE PSYC[illegible] OF ROMANTIC LOVE

Robert A. Johnson is a Jungian analyst in private practice in San Diego, California. He is a well-known lecturer and is the author of *He: Understanding Masculine Psychology* and *She: Understanding Feminine Psychology*, which have sold over 100,000 copies each. He has studied at the Jung Institute in Switzerland and at the Sri Aurobindo Ashram in India.

ROBERT A. JOHNSON

THE PSYCHOLOGY OF ROMANTIC LOVE

ARKANA
LONDON

First published in Great Britain in 1984
ARKANA edition 1987
ARKANA PAPERBACKS is an imprint of
Routledge & Kegan Paul Ltd
11 New Fetter Lane, London EC4P 4EE

ISBN 1–85063–077–1

Made and printed in Great Britain by
The Guernsey Press Co. Ltd., Guernsey, Channel Islands.

Contents

PART III

PART IV

CONCLUSION

A Note on the Sources and Translation of the Myth

This work is a Jungian interpretation of *Tristan and Iseult* that focuses on the symbols in the myth as sources of psychological insight. It is not intended to be a scholarly study of the myth as literature. Therefore, in order to maintain the flow of narrative and commentary, I have avoided footnote references throughout the text of the myth. Scholars and students of medieval literature will already know the sources of the material, and others would only be distracted from the real purpose of the book by a pretense of scholarly documentation.

Some readers may wish to read the myth in its entirety before returning to my commentary, contained in the chapters following each Narrative section. I have adapted the myth mainly from the famous Bédier compilation of the turn of the century, translated into English by Hilaire Belloc and Paul Rosenfeld. Of necessity I have condensed the material, but in many places where condensation would have bled the story of its energy and power, I have quoted both dialogue and narrative directly from the brilliant Belloc/Rosenfeld translation. (Such quotations are set off in italic type.) An example in point is the last scene of the story, in which Queen Iseult, landing from her ship, dashes to find Tristan: "*She went up to the palace, following the way, and her cloak was random and wild. . . .*" Thus begins one of the most beautiful passages ever rendered into English.

Whether scholar or layperson, all should read this marvelous translation in its entirety. It is a rare work of art, for it retains the magnificent simplicity and poetic imagery of archaic English but avoids the self-conscious, flowery affectations that bedevil most such efforts.

I have departed from Monsieur Bédier's version of the myth in only one significant detail: I take from Béroul, the first poet to tell the tale of Tristan, the period of three years that the love potion wields its magic power over the lovers. I feel that Béroul's version is closer to the archetypal soil, so to speak, from which the myth first grew.

A Note for Women

Women will find, in the story of Tristan and Iseult, a vivid symbolic picture of the huge forces at work in all of us, both men and women, when we are caught up in the experience of romantic love.

The myth not only records the dynamics of romantic love in the male psyche, it also reflects the fate of the feminine in our culture; it shows how the feminine values of feeling, relatedness, and soul consciousness have been virtually driven out of our culture by our partriarchal mentality. One of the most important insights in the myth for women is the degree to which most men unconsciously search for their lost feminine side, for the feminine values in life, and attempt to find their unlived feminine side through woman.

But it is not only men who have accepted the patriarchal version of reality. Women also have been taught to idealize masculine values at the expense of the feminine side of life. Many women have spent their lives in a constant feeling of inferiority because they felt that to be feminine was "second best." Women have been trained that only masculine activities, thinking, power, and achieving have any real value. Thus Western woman finds herself in the same psychological dilemma as Western man: developing a one-sided, competitive mastery of the masculine qualities at the expense of her feminine side.

Although this mythical evocation of romantic love is told from a man's standpoint and seen through a man's eyes, women will find much of their own experience in it. But a woman should bear in mind that the myth does not always necessarily reflect a woman's psychology or a woman's special way of experiencing romantic love. There are "women's myths," such as "Eros and Psyche" (for which see my book *She*), that present a more exact picture of woman's inner structure.

The psychological makeups of men and women are distinct. If we tried fully to explain a woman's psychology through a "man's myth," it would inevitably give a distorted view of her structure. This is especially true in romantic love, for a woman's feeling side develops differently than a man's, and her experience of relationship has subtle nuances that men do not experience in the same way.

Most women spend a tremendous part of their energy in efforts to make a loving relationship with a man and to deal with his seemingly incomprehensible feelings, ideas, and reactions. By making her own journey with Tristan and Iseult, she will understand better the "Tristan" in her life, and how to draw out the best in him. But also, and of equal importance, she will have a clearer view of her own unknown self.

Introduction

Romantic love is the single greatest energy system in the Western psyche. In our culture it has supplanted religion as the arena in which men and women seek meaning, transcendence, wholeness, and ecstasy.

As a mass phenomenon, romantic love is peculiar to the West. We are so accustomed to living with the beliefs and assumptions of romantic love that we think it is the only form of "love" on which marriage or love relationships can be based. We think it is the only "true love." But there is much that we can learn from the East about this. In Eastern cultures, like those of India or Japan, we find that married couples love each other with great warmth, often with a stability and devotion that puts us to shame. But their love is not "romantic love" as we know it. They don't impose the same ideals on their relationships, nor do they impose such impossible demands and expectations on each other as we do.

Romantic love is not just a form of "love," it is a whole psychological package—a combination of beliefs, ideals, attitudes, and expectations. These often contradictory ideas coexist in our unconscious minds and dominate our reactions and behavior, without our being aware of them. We have automatic assumptions about what a relationship with another person is, what we should feel, and what we should "get out of it."

For romantic love doesn't just mean loving someone; it means being "in love." This is a psychological phenomenon that is very specific. When we are "in love" we believe we have found the ultimate meaning of life, revealed in another human being. We feel we are finally completed, that we have found the missing parts of ourselves. Life suddenly seems to have a wholeness, a superhuman intensity that lifts us high above the ordinary plain of existence. For us, these are the sure signs of "true love." The psychological package includes an unconscious demand that our lover or spouse always provide us with this feeling of ecstasy and intensity.

With typical Western self-righteousness we assume that our notion of "love," romantic love, must be the best. We assume that any other kind of love between couples would be cold and insignificant by comparison. But if we Westerners are honest with ourselves, we have to admit that our approach to romantic love is not working well.

Despite our ecstasy when we are "in love," we spend much of our time with a deep sense of loneliness, alienation, and frustration over our inability to make genuinely loving and committed relationships. Usually we blame other people for failing us; it doesn't occur to us that perhaps it is we who need to change our own unconscious attitudes—the expectations and demands we impose on our relationships and on other people.

This is the great wound in the Western psyche. It is the primary psychological problem of our Western culture. Carl Jung said that if you find the psychic wound in an individual or a people, there you also find their path to consciousness. For it is in the healing of our psychic wounds that we come to know ourselves. Romantic love, if we truly undertake the task of understanding it, becomes such a path to consciousness. If Westerners will free themselves from their automatic servitude to their unconscious assumptions and expectations they will not only find a new awareness in their relationships but a new awareness of their own selves.

Romantic love has existed throughout history in many cultures. We find it in the literature of ancient Greece, the Roman Empire, ancient Persia, and feudal Japan. But our modern Western society is the only culture in history that has experienced romantic love as a mass phenomenon. We are the only society that makes romance the basis of our marriages and love relationships and the cultural ideal of "true love."

The ideal of romantic love burst into Western society during the Middle Ages. It first appeared in our literature in the myth of Tristan and Iseult, then in the love poems and songs of the troubadours. It was called "courtly love"; its model was the brave knight who worshiped a fair lady as his inspiration, the symbol of all beauty and perfection, the ideal that moved him to be noble, spiritual, refined, and high-minded. In our time we have mixed courtly love into our sexual relationships and marriages, but we still hold the medieval belief that true love has to be the ecstatic adoration of a man or woman who carries, for us, the image of perfection.

Carl Jung has shown us that when a great psychological phenomenon suddenly appears in the life of an individual, it represents a tremendous unconscious potential that is rising to the level of consciousness. The same is true for a culture. At a certain point in the history of a people, a new possibility bursts out of the collective unconscious; it is a new idea, a new belief, a new value, or a new way of looking at the universe. It represents a potential good if it can be integrated into consciousness, but at first it is overwhelming, even destructive.

Romantic love is one of these truly overwhelming

psychological phenomena that have appeared in Western history. It has overwhelmed our collective psyche and permanently altered our view of the world. As a society, we have not yet learned to handle the tremendous power of romantic love. We turn it into tragedy and alienation more often than into enduring human relationships. But, I believe, if men and women will understand the psychological dynamics behind romantic love and learn to handle them consciously, they will find a new possibility of relationship, both to themselves and to others.

Our vehicle for exploring romantic love is the myth of Tristan and Iseult. It is one of the most moving, beautiful, and tragic of all the great epic tales. It was the first story in Western literature that dealt with romantic love. It is the source from which all our romantic literature has sprung, from Romeo and Juliet down to the love story in the movie at the local cinema. By applying the principles of Jungian psychology, we will interpret the symbols in the myth and learn what it has to teach us about the origins, the nature, and the meaning of romantic love.

The myth of Tristan and Iseult, like that of Parsifal, is a "man's myth." It portrays the life of young Tristan, who grows into a noble and selfless hero and then meets the overwhelming experience of his life in his passion for Queen Iseult. It is a symbolic tapestry, picturing vividly the development of an individual male consciousness as he struggles to win his masculinity, to become conscious of his feminine side, and to deal with love and relatedness. It shows a man torn among the conflicting forces and loyalties that rage within the male psyche when he is consumed by the joys, the passions, and the sufferings of romance.

Nevertheless, there is much in this myth that is of great value and interest to women. For Tristan reveals also those universal dynamics of romantic love that are common to both men and women. (Please see A Note for Women.) To look at this myth, to experience it as a rich evocation of the Western psyche's journey, will help a woman not only to better understand a man in her life but to see more clearly the mysterious forces at work within her own self.

For both men and women, to look honestly at romantic love is a heroic journey. It forces us to look not only at the beauty and potential in romantic love but also at the contradictions and illusions we carry around inside us at the unconscious level. Heroic journeys always lead through dark valleys and difficult confrontations. But if we persevere, we find a new possibility of consciousness.

On Myths

My lords, if you would hear a high tale of love and of death, here is that of Tristan and Queen Iseult; how to their full joy, but to their sorrow also, they loved each other, and how at last, they died of that love together upon one day; she by him and he by her.

Thus begins the marvelous story of Tristan and Iseult. It was with these words that the traveling poets and minstrels of the Middle Ages would call together the lords and ladies, the knights and commonfolk, to hear a wondrous story of adventure and love. They would gather before the wood fire in the great hall of a castle or manor and relive together the "high tale" of the knight Tristan and his fatal love for Queen Iseult.

This story is one of the great myths of all time; it has the dignity and power of Gilgamesh, Beowulf, or the Icelandic sagas. Such myths have an uncanny power to thrill us, uplift us, pull us out of the pettiness of our ego-lives, and transport us to a realm of magic, noble deeds, and unearthly passion. But a myth does more than that: If we learn to listen, it also gives us specific psychological information and teaches the deep truths of the psyche.

Years ago a grammar school teacher asked her class, "What is a myth?" A young boy, the son of a couple whom I know well, raised his hand and replied, "A myth is something that is true on the inside, but not true on the outside." The teacher did not understand, but often children have more psychological wisdom than adults. A myth *is* true: It is not true in the outer, physical sense, but it is an accurate expression of a psychological situation, of the inner condition of the psyche.

Myths are like dreams. Dreams are the messengers of the unconscious mind. Through them the unconscious communicates its contents and its concerns to the conscious mind. By learning the symbolic language of dreams, a person learns to see what is going on within at an unconscious level and even discovers what needs to be done about it. Jung demonstrated that myths also are symbolic expressions of the unconscious. But, though a dream expresses the dynamics within an individual, a myth expresses the dynamics within the *collective* mind of a society, culture, or race.

A myth is the collective "dream" of an entire people at a certain point in their history. It is as though the entire population dreamed together, and that "dream," the myth, burst forth through its poetry, songs, and stories. But a myth not only lives in literature and imagination, it immediately finds its way into the behavior and attitudes of the culture—into the practical daily lives of the people.

The myth of Tristan and Iseult is a profound expression of the Western psyche. It tells us a lot about "what makes us tick." It is a vivid, panoramic view of the psychological forces at work in the unconscious of Western people for the last thousand years of our history. Above all, this myth gives us a painfully accurate picture of romantic love—why it came into our culture, what it is, and why it isn't working very well.

Our myth shows us that romantic love is a necessary ingredient in the evolution of the Western psyche. We will achieve wholeness and will move on to the next step in our evolution of consciousness only when we learn to live consciously with romantic love—that is, with the vast psychological forces that it represents. In the evolution of consciousness, our greatest problem is always our richest opportunity.

Zen teaches that inner growth always involves an experience of "a red-hot coal stuck in the throat." In our development we always come to a problem, an obstacle, that goes so deep that we "can't swallow it and can't cough it up." This exactly fits our Western experience of romantic love: We can't live with it, and we can't live without it—we can't swallow it, and can't cough it up! This "hot coal" in our throats alerts us that a tremendous evolutional potential is trying to manifest itself.

After many years of living in the rich world of the psyche and learning its laws, Carl Jung saw a vast evolutional Power at work in the psychic universe. He saw that the human psyche strives always toward wholeness, strives to complete itself and become more conscious. The unconscious mind seeks to move its contents up to the level of consciousness, where they can be actualized and assimilated into a more complete conscious personality. Each person's psyche has an inborn evolutional urge to grow, to integrate the contents of the unconscious, to bring together all the missing parts of the total individual into a complete, whole, and conscious self.

Jung teaches us that the unconscious is the *source:* the primal matter from which our conscious minds and ego personalities have evolved. All the values, ideas, feelings, capacities, and attitudes that we have developed into functioning parts of our conscious personalities originated in the raw, primal material of the unconscious.

To get a clear image of this, we may picture a coral island that gradually rises out of the sea. The ocean slowly creates this island out of its own matter and pushes it finally above the water into the sunlight. After centuries, topsoil and plant life develop, animals and people appear, and the little island becomes a tiny center of human life and consciousness. Like the vast ocean, the collective unconscious gives birth to a tiny island; it is the conscious psyche, the ego, the "I"—the part of me that is aware of itself.

This little ego-mind, surrounded by the vastness of the unconscious, has a high and noble task, a special destiny to live out. Its role in this evolution is to integrate more and more of the unconscious until the conscious mind truly reflects the wholeness of the self.

All humankind is in the grip of this huge evolutional Power. When the collective unconscious begins a new stage in this process, it tolerates no obstacle. In order to force a new ideal or possibility into the conscious psyche of a people, it will turn a society upside down, launch crusades, beget new religions, or shake empires down into rubble.

This vision of psychic evolution is crucial for us, both for understanding our myth and for seeing romantic love in true perspective. The appearance of romantic love in the West began a momentous chapter in this cosmic drama of evolution. Romantic love is the mask behind which a powerful array of new possibilities hides, waiting to be integrated into consciousness. But what has begun as a huge collective surge of psychic energy must be perfected at the *individual* level. It is always the role of individuals to complete the task, to bring the divine process to fruition within the microcosm of our own souls. It is up to us, as individuals, to take this raw unconscious energy of romantic love, this confusing array of impulses and possibilities, and transform it into awareness and relatedness.

Every great myth is the symbolic record of such a stage of growth in the life of a people. This explains why these powerful stories capture us so completely and go so deep in our feelings. Tristan and Iseult is a symbolic blueprint of our Western psyche at a critical turning point in our psychological development. It shows us the conflict and illusions, but also the potentialities, inherent in the situation.

Now we are going to look at this "high tale of love and death." From time to time in our story we will pause to learn to read the symbolic language of the blueprint and to learn how to receive the wisdom that this myth offers us.

PART I

THE NARRATIVE

How Tristan Was Born and Grew Up to Be a Great Knight

Long ago, in the days of King Arthur, Mark was King in Cornwall. Now Mark was a fair and good king, and all his subjects loved him for his justice and kindness. But those were evil times, for cruel enemies surrounded Mark and invaded his lands. But good King Rivalen of Lyonesse brought his army across from France, and by his help King Mark won a great victory. So grateful was he that he gave his only sister, Blanchefleur, to be wed to King Rivalen, in token of eternal friendship and alliance. Blanchefleur was like her name, which means "white flower": delicate, fair, and pale. A royal wedding was held in Tintagel Castle, and there a baby was conceived—and you will hear more of that fateful child, for he is Tristan.

Before long came grim news: King Rivalen's cities in Lyonesse were besieged by a treacherous tyrant, Duke Morgan. Rivalen set sail, with his new Queen Blanchefleur and with his army, and returned to his land to do battle. But after months of war, poor King Rivalen was caught in foul ambush and cruelly murdered by Morgan.

When Blanchefleur heard, she grew pallid and faint, and her life flowed out of her. She had no more desire to live on earth but only longed to join her husband in the other world. Yet she was heavy with child. She abided three days in sorrow and longing for death. And on the fourth day she brought forth a child and said:

"*Little son, I have longed a while to see you, . . . the fairest thing ever a woman bore. In sadness came I hither, in sadness did I bring forth, in sadness has your first feast day gone. And as by sadness you came into the world, your name shall be called Tristan; that is, the child of sadness.*"

Thus did she name her child, and kissed him, and then she died.

Now Lord Rohalt was the faithful Marshal of King Rivalen. And when he saw the war was lost, he surrendered the castles to Duke Morgan, and all the land of Lyonesse came under tyranny. But Rohalt hid the baby Tristan among his own sons, lest the wicked Duke Morgan murder the child.

Tristan grew fair and strong among the sons of Rohalt, but he did not know who he was, believing Rohalt to be his own father. As he grew, his faithful squire taught him all the arts of barony:

Lance and sword,
'Scutcheon and bow,
To cast stone quoits,
To leap wide dykes,
To hate each lie and felony,
To keep his word,
To sing and play the harp,
To do the hunter's craft.

Tristan rode as though he and his horse were one. He was loyal and brave, although only a boy, and he wielded his sword like a full-grown knight. All men praised Rohalt for his noble son; but Rohalt looked on Tristan and knew him for his king.

One day Norwegian pirates, posing as merchants, lured Tristan aboard their ship. Though the boy fought like a lion cub, the pirates captured and bound him, for they could sell so fine a youth in servitude in some distant land. But the sea would not bear the felon ship. A terrible storm blew, and great waves poured over the decks. As the felons knew the gods of the ocean were angered by their crime, they put Tristan into a boat and set him free. Instantly the waves calmed. Ahead Tristan saw land, and he gratefully pulled for shore. Now those were the fair green shores of Cornwall, and there his uncle, King Mark, still ruled.

By chance the King's huntsmen were by the shore, and Tristan so pleased them by his skill that they took him to the court of the King. But when Mark gazed on Tristan he was troubled and filled with tenderness, and knew not why. For in Tristan he saw the face of his beloved sister, Blanchefleur, and her blood called out to him.

After the evening meal Tristan took up a harp and sang the old songs. Then every heart was lifted and every eye filled with tears, and King Mark said:

"Son, blessed be the master that taught thee, and blessed be thou of God: for God loves good singers. . . . For our joy did you come to this roof, stay near us a long time, friend!"

And Tristan answered: "Here will I stay, my lord, and serve you faithfully as your liege." For three years Tristan lived in Tintagel Castle, and the King was as a father to him, and a deep love grew between them.

When three years had passed, the faithful Marshal Rohalt came to Cornwall, for he had searched for Tristan in many lands. Thus Tristan found out who he was: the nephew of King Mark, the son of King Rivalen, the heir to the throne of Lyonesse. Then, with a company of good knights, Tristan crossed the waters to Lyonesse and raised the countryside, and the people rose with courage against the tyrant Morgan. Tristan met the traitor on the field of combat and slew him with the sword, and thus he repaid Morgan's treachery in times past.

But Tristan put Rohalt on the throne of Lyonesse and said to his barons:

"Here I am King, and this land is dear, but my heart is with my uncle, good King Mark. Now the tyrant is dead, I give you here my faithful Rohalt, to rule you in my stead. For I must up and go to Mark, and serve him as my lord."

At those words the barons groaned and cried together, for they would keep Tristan in Lyonesse, to rule them. But they answered: "It is just, my lord."

In those days Ireland was a mighty kingdom, and the Irish King taxed Cornwall for a terrible tribute. The Cornish people ground their teeth together in anger and sorrow, for every fourth year they had to send three hundred youths and three hundred maidens, of their sons and daughters, to serve as slaves and die in Ireland. But for fifteen years King Mark had refused to pay the tribute, and the Irish King was wrathful. Now the Queen in Ireland was a great sorceress, and her brother was a giant, called the Morholt. So tall and strong was he that not even five knights together could overcome him.

One sad day the Morholt landed in Cornwall with many knights and demanded the tribute of youths and maidens.

"But," said he, "if any knight in Cornwall will fight me, then will we have a trial by combat to see if the King of Ireland receives his tribute without cause. For God will give me the victory if my Irish King is in the right!"

The Morholt stood before all the barons in the King's court and offered trial by combat. But all stood silent and afraid. Again, the next day, he came before the King's court and offered combat. But it was as though a hawk had entered into a cage of sparrows: The Cornish barons shivered and hid their heads under their wings. But on the third day, a young boy stood forth and, kneeling before the King, said: "My lord, let me do battle." And that boy was Tristan.

Tristan fought the Morholt on a tiny islet off the shore. On the day of battle, the barons cried with pity and shame, for they had not Tristan's courage. The people followed Tristan to the shore, weeping and praying. *They still had hope, for hope in the heart of men lives on lean pasture.*

At the battleground Tristan jumped from his boat; then he turned and pushed his boat adrift. The Morholt was surprised, but Tristan said: "One of us only will go hence alive; one boat will serve."

The people gathered on the shore heard three times a great cry from the islet. The knights of the Morholt laughed, sure of victory. But the Cornish women wept and did rituals of mourning, standing in a line, clapping their hands in unison, making a high-pitched mourning wail.

At noontime the people saw the Morholt's boat returning from the islet, the wind billowing its sail of royal purple. Then truly they lost hope and wept in despair. But as the boat approached, suddenly they saw Tristan standing in the bow, holding two swords, and the sun gleamed on his armor. The young men cried out and jumped into the water in their joy, and swam out to meet him. Then, when they had pulled his boat in, Tristan said to the Morholt's knights:

"*My lords of Ireland, the Morholt fought well. See here, my sword is broken and a splinter of it stands fast in his head. Take you that steel, my lords; it is the tribute of Cornwall.*"

Though blood flowed from his wounds, Tristan walked through Tintagel town, up to the castle. The crowds waved green branches and spread flowers along his path; they shouted praises to God; they hung rich tapestries from their windows; and all along the way bells pealed and trumpets sounded in joy. Before the castle Tristan fell in the arms of King Mark and fainted from his wounds.

Tristan's wounds grew worse and worse, for the Morholt had pierced him with a poisoned barb. He turned pale and his body wasted; neither doctor nor magician could they find to heal him. For that poison only the sorceress Queen of Ireland, and her daughter, Iseult the Fair, had the secret charms of healing. But those two magical women were in Ireland. Day and night they watched over the body of the Morholt; day and night they cursed the name of Tristan of Lyonesse; day and night they thirsted for revenge.

Now Tristan knew there was no cure for him in Cornwall. But his heart told him to go to sea and seek there either healing or death.

"I would like to try the sea that brings all chances. . . . I would have the sea bear me far off alone, to what land no matter, so that it heal me of my wound. And perchance some day I will once more serve you, fair uncle, as your harper, your huntsman, and your liege."

They laid him gently in a small boat, without sail or oars. He left his sword on the shore, for it could no longer help him. But he took his harp into the boat for comfort on the way. Then, with tears, they pushed him out to sea and committed him to God. And the sea drew him away . . .

For seven days and seven nights Tristan lay upon the waters, and then he drew near a shore. In the darkness of night, fishermen heard soft melodies like silver, floating above the water. At dawn they found him, lifeless in his boat, his hand resting on his silent harp. The fishermen took Tristan ashore and sent instant word to their lady, for she had the gift of healing.

Their lady was Iseult the Fair; her mother was the sorceress Queen of Ireland, and this harbor was Whitehaven, where the Morholt lay in his tomb. So they carried the wounded stranger to the Princess Iseult. Of all the women in the world, she alone could heal him. But of all the women in the world, it was she who most wished him dead.

1

Blanchefleur

We will leave Tristan in Ireland for now, and pause for a while. Now is the time to begin to look at the symbolic language of our myth, to begin to understand the truths it has to teach us.

At the beginning we find a hero born in sadness, his mother lost on the first day of his earthly life. But who is this child? What does Blanchefleur's death mean for us?

The loss of Tristan's mother is not his experience alone. For Tristan is the prototype of modern Western man, the firstborn of our modern race. Tristan's mind is our mind, his world is our world, his problems are our problems, and his loss is our loss.

Psychologically our modern era began in the twelfth century, the time when Tristan was born and this myth came to life. That century was a great watershed in our history. The seeds of our modern mind were planted in that time: What we are today—our attitudes, values, conflicts, and ideals—has grown from those seeds. The collective psyche is like a giant spreading tree that grows slowly, century by century. For this huge, evolving, collective mind, a thousand years is but a short time.

Tristan is the new child, born in the Middle Ages, who grew up over a millennium to be modern Western man. His mother and father, Blanchefleur and King Ri-

valen, symbolize the old order, the ancient mind of Europe. They die, but they give birth to a child, and that child is the modern mind of the West. He is Tristan, the New Man.

Blanchefleur's tragic death leaves Tristan in a sadly distorted world, bereft of almost all traces of the feminine. And like Tristan, we have inherited that world. For Blanchefleur is the inner feminine. She personifies the inner feminine soul of Western man, the feminine values that once lived in our culture. Her death records that sad day in our history when our patriarchal mentality finally drove the feminine completely out of our culture and out of our individual lives.

Tristan is raised to the "arts of barony." And what are those? To fight with the sword, the lance, and the bow. To ride a war-horse and leap wide dykes. To hunt. Everything in his world emphasizes the masculine side of life: wielding power, training for battle, defending territory. Every hero needs these skills—of that be sure! But they represent only half of human nature. King Mark has no queen; his sister, Blanchefleur has died. The whole feminine side of life—love, feeling relationship, introspection, the intuitive and lyrical experience of life—has all but disappeared from Cornwall and Lyonesse. The only remnant of the feminine left to Tristan is his harp, but as we shall see, it is his harp that saves him.

We will understand our story better if we get a clear idea of what we mean by "the feminine."

Jung found that the psyche is *androgynous:* It is made up of both masculine and feminine components. Thus, every man and every woman comes equipped with a psychological structure that in its wholeness includes the richness of both sides, both natures, both sets of capacities and strengths. The psyche spontaneously divides itself into complementary opposites and represents them as a

masculine-feminine constellation. It characterizes some qualities as being "masculine" and certain others as being "feminine." Like *yin* and *yang* in ancient Chinese psychology, these complementary opposites balance and complete each other. No human value or trait is complete in itself: It must be joined with its masculine or feminine "mate" in a conscious synthesis if we are to have balance and wholeness.

The psyche sees our capacity for relatedness and love as a "feminine" quality, emanating from the feminine side of the psyche. By contrast it views the ability to wield power, control situations, and defend territory as strengths that we find in the "masculine" department of the psyche. To become a complete man or woman, each of us must develop both sides of the psyche. We must be able both to handle power and to love, both to exert control and to flow spontaneously with fate—each value in its season.

When we speak of "feminine" in this sense, we obviously do not mean "pertaining to women." We are speaking of inner, psychological qualities that are common to both men and women. When a man develops the strengths of his inner feminine, it actually completes his maleness. He becomes more fully male as he becomes more fully human. The strongest man is the one who can genuinely show love to his children, as well as fight his battles in the business world during the work day. His masculine strength is augmented and balanced by his feminine capacity to be related, to express his affection and his feelings.

In each of us there is a potential for wholeness, for bringing the conflicting parts of ourselves together in a synthesis. We have a simple name for this totality of the individual: Jung called it the "self."

The *self* is the sum of all the divergent forces, ener-

gies, and qualities that live within you and make you who you are—a unique individual. The self is the balanced, harmonious, symmetrical unity at the very center of one's being, which each of us senses within. But we rarely experience the self with our conscious mind; we rarely have that sense of unity and wholeness. We feel ourselves usually as a chaotic mass of conflicting desires, values, ideals, and possibilities, some conscious and some unconscious, pulling us in many directions at once.

The work of "enlightenment" is to make conscious these divided and conflicting parts of ourselves, to wake up to the primordial unity that joins them. To awaken to the unity of the self is the great goal of our psychological evolution, the Pearl Without Price, the object of our deepest longings. It is this possibility that is manifested by the dual masculine-feminine nature of the psyche.

In mythical symbolism the self is often represented by a masculine-feminine pair: a king and queen, a divine brother and sister, a god and goddess. Through this symbol of the royal couple the psyche tells us that the self is one, though we experience it as complementary opposites. It shows us that we must make a "marriage," a holy synthesis, between the two great polarities of our human nature. Like the dragons of *yin* and *yang,* the inner king and queen constantly create our world out of the masculine and feminine energies of the self in an eternal cosmic dance.

But Tristan's world has no queen! There is a king: There is Mark. But the queen has died: Blanchefleur has gone away.

It is the feminine qualities that bring meaning into life: relatedness to other human beings, the ability to soften power with love, awareness of our inner feelings and values, respect for our earthly environment, a delight in earth's beauty, and the introspective quest for inner wisdom. With these qualities shortchanged, we don't find much meaning. With our swords and lances we build our empires, but they don't give us a sense of meaning or purpose.

But the death of Blanchefleur does not mean that we have lost these qualities forever. Death, in a myth or dream, means something has left the conscious mind; yet it rests in the unconscious, waiting to be reborn into consciousness. We see people today trying to bring Blanchefleur back from the unconscious. People try to learn to express their feelings, to show affection, to awaken to the intuitive side of life. Some of it misfires, becomes a fad, is reduced to self-conscious embraces and forced "spontaneity," but at least people are trying to find Blanchefleur.

Why did Blanchefleur die? Why have we Western people lost so much of our capacity to love, to feel, to be related?

Look at Blanchefleur! She is surrounded by war, married to an ally for help in a war, rushed to another war in Lyonesse that kills her husband and destroys her will to live. Ever a camp follower, she only knows of soldiers, battles, alliances, and death. In our culture the inner feminine is the same—always a camp follower, dragged in the dusty train of masculine power drive, choked by war, forgotten in a deafening and eternal clash of steel.

When Blanchefleur died, that cold day in Lyonesse, the feminine soul of the West departed: to Ireland, to some mythical island across the seas. She went to live in the unconscious, to await a better time when she will return to human life.

2

The Child of Sadness

"In sadness came I hither, in sadness did I bring forth, and in sadness has your first feast day gone. And as by sadness you came into the world, your name shall be called Tristan; that is, the child of sadness."

The world of King Mark, King Rivalen, and Duke Morgan is a vivid symbol of our patriarchal mind. None of us is fully aware of how much he or she is dominated by patriarchal prejudices. None of us is fully awake to how much the masculine pursuit of power, production, prestige, and "accomplishment" impoverishes us and drives the feminine values out of our lives.

Like Tristan, we are the children of sadness. Western people are children of inner poverty, though outwardly we have everything. Probably no other people in history have been so lonely, so alienated, so confused over values, so neurotic. We have dominated our environment with sledge-hammer force and electronic precision. We amass riches on an unprecedented scale. But few of us, very few indeed, are at peace with ourselves, secure in our relationships, content in our loves, or at home in the world. Most of us cry out for meaning in life, for values we can live by, for love and relationship.

Our sadness results from the loss of those feminine values that we have denigrated and driven out of our culture. Blanchefleur could not survive in a culture that only honors acquisition, power, competition, and "looking out for number one." The very beginning of our myth tells us what kind of world we have been building, the world Tristan is born into. There is constant war; men think only of empire building, accumulation of territory and wealth, and domination of the environment at any cost. We still call it progress. But this lopsided mentality kills Rivalen and Blanchefleur and leaves Tristan an orphan.

King Rivalen's marriage with Blanchefleur symbolizes our Western attempt to make a synthesis within the patriarchal mentality. But it can't survive, for it is based on our assumption that feminine values must always be subservient to masculine demands for power. Finally, Duke Morgan, the end result of patriarchal attitudes, destroys that frail synthesis: He kills the King and Queen.

Blanchefleur was never given her rightful place in that society; the values she represented were never respected in their own right. Though Mark loves his sister, he trades her off to Rivalen for help in defending his territory, to seal their alliance. She is a piece of property, to be used as the masculine ego sees fit in the service of its power drive. If we are awake, we see this in our own society. When a man uses a woman's feelings to get power over her, when a man starts a friendship only so he can sell something to his friend, when the advertiser on television tells us that we will buy his product if we "really love our children," each of them is cynically putting love and feeling in the service of power and profit. As a society, we keep trading Blanchefleur away.

Duke Morgan represents the ultimate extreme, the final degradation, of the patriarchal mentality. When King Rivalen's back is turned, he attacks. He lies in wait, and murders. He builds nothing positive; he only plunders. Duke Morgan symbolizes the masculine half of the psyche that has lost all contact with the inner feminine; he is a power drive gone mad without the balancing force of love, feeling, and human values. He seeks only power; he destroys all that is human and tender; he is reduced to brutality.

In our own time we do not have to look far to find Duke Morgan. We find him running governments, corporations, and even households. If we look honestly, we find traces of him within our own selves, for he is universal. When we denigrate the inner feminine and lose touch with her values, we become like Duke Morgan. We spend our days thinking only of how to get ahead, how to win, how to find a better position in business and society, how to make our families and friends do exactly what we want them to do. We forget how to be true to our own values, to our inner selves, to the people we love.

The specter of Duke Morgan awakens us to a profound psychological reality: *No aspect of the human psyche can live in a healthy state unless it is balanced by its complementary opposite.* If the masculine mind tries to live without its "other half," the feminine soul, then the masculine becomes unbalanced, sick, and finally monstrous. Power without love becomes brutality. Feeling without masculine strength becomes woolly sentimentality.

When one side of human nature grows out of balance with the other, it becomes a tyranny in the soul. That is the tyrant Duke Morgan. It drives its complementary opposite into the unconscious. That is Blanchefleur. But the unconscious will not tolerate this kind of imbalance; we have already learned that the greatest force in the psychic universe is the demand for completion, for wholeness, for balance. The feminine will return. Across the seas Iseult is waiting. And when Iseult comes, the self-satisfied patriarchal world will never be the same.

So there is hope for the child of sadness. Tristan is also the child of hope. The child as a symbol always represents a new possibility, a new consciousness that has been born into the human psyche. Tristan inherited a sad world, but he also inherited inner strength, the potential for making a new world and a new understanding. Tristan is a hero. He will go forth and defeat Duke Morgan. He will regain his birthright. And he will find Iseult, the reincarnation of Blanchefleur. We are Tristan; Tristan is Everyman. We have his sadness, we have his challenges, and we have his hope.

3

Islands of Consciousness, Seas of God

Sail forth—steer for the deep waters only,
Reckless O Soul, exploring, I with thee, and thou with me,
For we are bound where mariner has not yet dared to go,
And we will risk the ship, ourselves and all.

O my brave soul!
O farther, farther sail!
O daring joy, but safe! are they not all the seas of God?
O farther, farther, farther sail!

—*Walt Whitman,* Passage to India

For all humankind and through all the ages, the sea has been the great symbol of the unconscious. The islands across the sea, the exotic kingdoms and distant lands, have always represented the Great Unknown. Our longing for these places of mystery, magic, flying carpets, and genies has a deep inner meaning. It is our nostalgia for the mysterious, unexplored depths of our own psyches, for the hidden potentialities within our own souls: for what we have never known, never lived, never dared.

In Tristan's time, the world was small. The exotic, unknown land on the other side of the sea was Ireland. It was in Ireland that you found a sorceress queen, a legendary princess, dragons, and giants. In Walt Whitman's day the mystical, uncharted realm of the unconscious was symbolized by India, and a passage to India was that heroic journey to the unconscious "where mariner has not yet dared to go." In our century we have yet another myth, another symbol. Spaceships bring extraterrestrial beings from far-off galaxies and planets, civilizations more advanced and powerful than our own, from which we learn new and wondrous things.

Each of these mythical maps depicts the human psyche. The ego lives on its tiny island of Cornwall, that little part of the vast psychic universe that it knows. But across the sea or the unconscious, across the vast reaches of interstellar space, are other "islands of consciousness," with their own values, their own strengths, their own points of view. With these centers of consciousness the ego needs to make a synthesis.

Cornwall is the island of the ego, dominated by the patriarchal masculine attitude. Ireland is the island of the unconscious matriarchal feminine, dominated by the sorceress Queen. Neither of these can live without its complementary opposite. Cornwall must go to Ireland, or Ireland will come to Cornwall.

The unconscious unceasingly pulls Tristan toward Ireland, for Tristan is the hero who must pull the islands together. He must launch forth on these seas of God and go where "mariner has not yet dared to go."

Even the pirates are in the service of this evolution. When the time comes for the ego to set forth on its journey toward wholeness, strange and paradoxical things happen; fate chooses strange emissaries. To be kidnapped by pirates seemed a horrible disaster. But when we grow wiser we learn that the disasters of life are often the genius of the unconscious, forcing our egos into a new experience of the self. Thus Fate, disguised as a filthy pirate reeking of rum and blood, drags Tristan out onto the waters and forces him on to the next port in his journey of evolution.

Of course, there is a fight between Cornwall and Ireland. The inner attempt at synthesis always begins with conflict. So when we first hear of Ireland we also hear of *tribute,* and a terrible one—three hundred youths and three hundred maidens! Now, what does this mean?

If a man or woman clings to the dominant patriarchal attitude and refuses to make peace with the inner feminine, then she will demand a tribute: When we refuse to integrate a powerful new potentiality from the unconscious, the unconscious will exact a tribute, one way or another. The "tribute" may take the form of a neurosis, a compulsive mood, hypochondria, obsessions, imaginary illnesses, or a paralyzing depression. In his writings Carl Jung gives us a vivid example. His patient was a brilliant intellectual, a scientist. The man tried to exist without feelings, without emotional relationships, without a religious life. He suddenly developed an obsessive belief in a stomach cancer. The cancer did not exist, physically, yet he suffered all the terrors of hell. The obsession paralyzed him and his professional life. His orderly, rational mind could not solve the problem. He found relief from this obsession only when he consented to reintegrate the feminine side of his psyche, the human values and spiritual values he had discarded many years before. That is the Morholt! That is the Morholt exacting tribute at the point of the sword.

If only we would learn to honor the feminine side. If only we knew how to go to Ireland and make peace! Instead, we try to live out the feminine side in compulsive, unconscious ways: We eat and drink too much, we get captured by moods, we have headaches. If we learned to live the Feminine in a more conscious way, the sales of aspirin would fall drastically. We need to learn to take a walk in the sunshine and see the colors of the earth, to respect our physical bodies, to wake up to the music in life, to listen to our dreams, to show affection to the people we love. Then we can make peace; we will no longer find the Morholt at our doors, no longer find the sword at our throats.

We don't do this by sitting rooted in our patriarchal attitudes, secure in Cornwall. We have to go to the parts of ourselves that we have barely touched, that we barely know. We must sail forth and steer for the deep waters, risking all, yet strangely safe upon those seas of God.

4

The Sword and the Harp

Tristan is simultaneously the ego of Western man, the "I" that is experiencing this story, and the figure of the hero. This has deep significance for us. For Western man the ego needs to be heroic. It is only the heroic spirit that lifts us above petty egocentricity, that puts us in the service of a higher ideal, that outfits us for our evolutional task.

The job of the hero is specific: to undertake the inner journey, to face the dragons and giants there, to find the hidden treasure. The external role of hero is less and less relevant in our time. Exterior castles to storm and dragons to slay are in short supply. But the most heroic task of all can be undertaken by any person, regardless of his or her external circumstances. Anyone can make the inner quest and take on the burden of becoming whole.

Two things are required for a hero: a sword and a harp. Our entire story thus far has been the interplay between the sword power and the harp power in Tristan. Tristan needed his sword to do battle, first with the wicked Duke Morgan, then with the brutal Morholt. The sword symbolizes the sharp, aggressive wielding of masculine power. With the sword a hero approaches the world aggressively, takes control of the situation, takes a strong position, defeats the adversary. On the level of the mind, the sword is the discriminating intellect that divides and analyzes. It figuratively "cuts through" problems and ideas to understand them; it is the logical, critical faculty in the mind.

Each of us needs the sword power. There are times when we need to be logical and analytical. At times we must be assertive and strong. But there are also times when neither logic nor force will avail; then we need to turn to the harp.

After the battle with the Morholt, when Tristan is wounded and the sword no longer serves him, he lays it down and takes up his harp. It is his harp that accompanies him on the waters. The harp is the lyrical, feeling side, corresponding to the inner feminine. With his harp power he shows feeling, expresses love, and makes relationship. It was by his harp power that Tristan awakened the love between him and his uncle. When he heard the harp, King Mark cried, "For our joy did you come to this roof, stay near us a long time, friend!"

The harp represents the power to develop a sense of values, to affirm what is good and true, to appreciate the beautiful; the harp enables a hero to put the sword in the service of a noble ideal. Our story shows us that it is the harp that enables us to journey on the seas of the unconscious.

To be complete, the hero must have both. Without the sword, the harp becomes ineffectual. But without the harp, the sword is reduced to egotistical brute force. People confuse these two powers more in relationship than in any other area of human life. We often hear a man and woman trying to "settle things" by arguing, criticizing each other, talking logic, poking holes in each other's arguments, splitting hairs. Then they wonder why all the spontaneous feeling of love and warmth has gone out of their marriage or their time together! These kinds of negotiations are always "sword" activity; people are talking sword talk.

The sword can not build relationship: it can't settle anything, it can't bind together. It can only rip apart. If you want to heal your relationship, build relationship, then you must learn to use the language of the harp. You must affirm the other person, express your love and feeling and devotion. This is an absolute law: The harp heals and binds together; the sword wounds and cuts asunder.

Tristan's victory over the Morholt is a profound lesson in the *correct* use of the sword. We need to pay attention. The Morholt represents the terrible force—the primitive, raw power—that the unconscious feminine unleashes against the masculine ego that tries to shut her out. Once the Morholt appears on the scene, this is no longer a courtship; it is deadly warfare. The unconscious feminine not only demands a place in a man's life; she demands absolute control. She demands that Tristan pay the tribute and be subject to her spell.

That would be an extreme swing from the one-sided patriarchal attitude to an equally unbalanced feminine attitude. It would be no marriage, no synthesis: It would be an enslavement to the opposite extreme of domination by the feminine. If a man surrenders and pays her tribute, or if his ego is destroyed in the battle with the Morholt, then he loses his masculinity and becomes a slave to his feminine side.

We see this in some men at certain stages of life. A man who has always been tough, an aggressive go-getter, will suddenly be attacked by his bottled-up feminine side. It may take the form of an illness, a depression, a loss of interest in life. Suddenly he is moody, hyperemotional, indecisive. His wife has to make his decisions for him while he retreats into moods and hypochondria.

A great paradox is laid out before us at this point in

our story. Before a masculine ego makes peace with the feminine, before it makes a marriage of the opposites, it first has to do battle with the Morholt. A man must first protect himself against the raw power plays of the inner feminine. He must develop enough masculine ego strength so that he can approach the powerful inner feminine on equal terms.

Many Western people, caught up in misunderstandings of Eastern religions or philosophy, make an ideal of getting rid of the ego. We need to understand that the ego is absolutely necessary; it has a vital role to play in the great drama of evolving consciousness. The ego has the specific task of going to the inner "Ireland," of making the synthesis among the different centers of consciousness within the vast universe of the psyche. For that task, the male ego needs to be a hero, like Tristan. And the hero's first task is to strengthen his masculine consciousness.

This is correct swordsmanship in a man. He must have sword power to protect his conscious life, as he must have harp power for his journey into the unconscious.

After Tristan's wonderful victory over the Morholt, there is great rejoicing. We remember that the people shouted with joy, the bells sounded to proclaim the victory. This is what goes on inside a man when he overcomes the Morholt and thus wins his masculinity; there is a great feeling of liberation, of triumph over the forces that would have made him weak or dependent. But even as a man rejoices, he is already defeated: The poison barb is in him.

This is a terrible trick of fate! Right triumphs over wrong. The children are saved by Tristan's courage. What cruel destiny stabs Tristan with the poisoned barb? It is required to get Tristan to Ireland. Without it, Tristan will never go to Iseult the Fair. Without it, Tristan will simply return to the one-sided, patriarchal mentality of Cornwall, congratulating himself on his masculine superiority, and never think of approaching the feminine again. The poison barb shows us that there is no final victory over the inner feminine: In every victory there will be a poisoned barb, defeat seeping through his veins even as he celebrates. This is what forces a man finally to drop his arrogance and go voluntarily to the feminine.

Tristan shows us how to surrender, at the right time and in the right way. He lays aside his sword, puts himself in a boat without sail or oar, takes only his harp, and casts himself adrift on the sea.

There comes a time in life when a man's ego doesn't have the answers. He doesn't know enough; he doesn't have the resources needed to resolve an impossible situation. Wherever Tristan searched, no one in Cornwall could heal his sickness. At such times a man must relinquish control. He needs to remember Tristan's words: "I would like to try the sea that brings all chances. . . . To what land no matter, so that it heal me of my wound." He needs to give himself over to the unconscious and drift with its tides until he finds an island of new consciousness for that era of his life.

One of the great strengths of the inner feminine is the ability to let go, to give up ego control, to stop trying to control the people and the situation, to turn the situation over to fate and wait on the natural flow of the universe. To give up the oar and sail means to drop personal control and give oneself over to the will of God. To leave the sword means to stop trying to understand by intellect or logic, to stop trying to force things. To take up the harp means to wait patiently, listening to a soft voice within, for the wisdom that comes not from logic or action but from feeling, intuition, the irrational and the lyrical.

We see Tristan cast upon the sea. We hear the sound

of a harp floating above the waves. Drawn by a power that is high above the understanding of his ego, with no human chart to guide him, Tristan comes at last to Ireland. And there Iseult awaits him.

PART II

THE NARRATIVE

How Tristan Was Conquered by the Wine of Love

Now we return to the story of Tristan. When last we saw him he was in Ireland. The fishermen had found him adrift in his boat, pulled him in to shore, and carried him to the palace of Iseult the Fair. Though he was ravaged by illness and fever, the Princess saw he was of noble blood and finely arrayed. While he slept, Iseult and her mother, the sorceress Queen, applied secret herbs, potions, and spells; in time Tristan felt healing course through his body. So changed was he by the poison that none of the Morholt's knights knew him, and Tristan said naught of who he was or whence he came. As soon as he had strength to journey he stole away, found passage across the waters, and returned to Cornwall, where the King and court received him with astonished joy.

But Tristan had enemies in Cornwall. Four felon barons envied and hated him, for he was the most famous of knights in that land and the most beloved of the people, and the King had made him heir to the throne. Those felons went among the other barons and said, "Tristan must be a sorcerer. Else how could he have defeated the giant? and magically cured himself of that poison? and returned from sure death on the sea? If he becomes King then will we hold our lands of a warlock!"

So the barons turned against Tristan, for few men

know that what wizards do by magic, some men do by goodness, love, and courage. All the barons came before King Mark and said he must take a queen and produce an heir of his body; else they would all rise in rebellion. The king was perplexed and secretly meditated ways to save the throne for Tristan.

One day two sparrows flew in a window in Tintagel Castle; they dropped a woman's golden hair, long and bright, into the astonished king's outstretched hand. Then Mark called the barons together and said he would have for his queen none other than the damsel of that golden hair, for he hoped thereby to put off the baron's demands. But Tristan was shamed, and to prove he did not covet the throne, he stood forth and vowed to find the lady with the hair of gold.

"The search is perilous, but I would put my life into peril for you, that your barons may know I love you loyally. I take this oath, to die on the adventure or to bring back the Queen with that fair hair."

But Tristan, when he saw that strand of hair, smiled to himself, for he remembered Iseult the Fair, and he already knew whose golden hair it was.

Tristan made ready his ship and sailed to Ireland. His crew trembled; for ever since the death of the Morholt, the Irish King hanged every Cornish sailor he captured. In Whitehaven Tristan pretended to be a merchant and awaited his chance to win the Princess Iseult. Then one day came the roaring of a terrible dragon, ravaging the Irish countryside, and the King of Ireland offered his daughter, Iseult, to marry the knight who defeated that dragon. Now, when Tristan heard this, he lost no time, but swiftly put on armor and mounted his stallion and went to fight.

So fierce was the beast that Tristan's lance broke against it, and his horse was killed by the dragon's fiery breath. Tristan plunged his sword deep into the soft underthroat, where it has no scales, and the monster fell dead. Iseult found Tristan, wounded and poisoned, close by the dragon's smoking corpse. So once again Iseult nursed Tristan with healing herbs and drew him back from the edge of death.

One day Iseult and her ladies made Tristan a hot bath of herbs. As Tristan sat contented in the water, she began to burnish his shield, clean dragon blood off his sword, and do such duties as a maiden owes a guest. Suddenly her eyes went to a small notch in the blade. Her head swam and she trembled. She went to find that splinter of steel she had taken from the head of her uncle, the Morholt, which she kept in a sacred reliquary. And she fitted that steel to the notch in Tristan's sword. Crying out, "You are that same Tristan, murderer of my uncle!" she lifted his own sword to strike him dead. But Tristan spoke calming words, and Iseult, torn between hope of love and vows of revenge, paused to listen.

"*King's daugher, . . . one day two swallows flew, and flew to Tintagel and bore one hair out of all your hairs of gold, and I thought they brought me good will and peace, so I came to find you over seas. So I braved the monster and his poison. See here, amid the threads of gold upon my coat your hair is sewn: the threads are tarnished, but your bright hair still shines.*"

When Iseult heard these words she lowered the sword. She went to look upon his coat of arms and found there her own hair of gold. She was silent for a long time. Then she kissed him on the lips.

A few days hence Tristan stood before the King and Queen of Ireland, and all the Irish lords, and revealed who he was and offered rich gifts from King Mark. He told them he slew the dragon to pay them a blood-fine for the Morholt. He offered that Iseult be King Mark's bride and Queen of Cornwall, that there be a perpetual alliance and peace between the two kingdoms and an end to war. Now the King and his barons were glad to hear these words and to receive these gifts, and glad for the honor to the Princess Iseult.

But *Iseult the Fair trembled for shame and anguish. Thus Tristan, having won her, disdained her; the fine story of the hair of gold was but a lie; it was to another he was delivering her. . . . So, for the love of King Mark, did Tristan by guile and by force conquer the Queen of the hair of gold. . . .*

He had come to Ireland, he the ravisher . . . with guile he had torn her from her mother and her land; he had not deigned to keep her for himself, and now he was carrying her away as his prey, over the waves, to the land of the enemy.

The sorceress Queen gathered flowers and herbs and roots; she steeped them in wine and over that potion cast a magic spell, and this was its power: They who drink of it together shall love each other with their every single sense and every thought, but its power will wane after a span of three years. Then she gave it secretly to Iseult's maid Brangien and charged her to offer it only to King Mark and Iseult on the night of their wedding, after they were alone.

When all preparations were made, Iseult went on board Tristan's ship, and they set sail for Cornwall. But the winds failed; they dropped anchor by a small island, and all went ashore save Tristan and Iseult and a servant child.

Then Tristan heard Iseult, alone in her tent on the deck, weeping pitifully and mourning her lost homeland. So he came to her, and spoke to her softly and sought to comfort her. But she turned her face from him, and would answer but few words.

Now the sun was burning hot, and they called for something to drink. The little servant girl searched, and in a secret place she found a pitcher of cool wine, which she set before them. They drank deeply of the brew, for they were thirsty.

Hours later Brangien the maid found Tristan and Iseult still seated there, staring into each other's eyes, entranced and spellbound. She saw the pitcher set before them and cold fear ran through her, for that was the vessel of the wine of herbs.

For two days the love potion flowed in Tristan's veins and he suffered the agonies of love, now as though pierced by sharp thorns, now as though surrounded with sweet, fragrant flowers, and always the image of Iseult floated before his eyes. Finally, on the third day, he went to her tent on the deck.

"Come in, my lord," she said.

"But why call me your lord," asked he, "when truly you are my queen?"

"Nay," she said, "for it is I—and against my will—am truly become your slave. If only you had never come to our shores! If only I had let you die and never healed you! But then I did not know. . . . I did not know how I should be tormented night and day."

Tristan stared at her as though at a vision of light. "Iseult," he whispered, "what did you not know? Iseult, what torments you?"

"The love of you," she said. Then he kissed her mouth and held her tight against him. Brangien came upon them so, and cried:

"*Stay and return if still you can. . . . But oh! that path has no returning. For already Love and his strength drag you on and now henceforth forever never shall you know joy without pain again . . . for through me and in that cup, you have drunk not love alone, but love and death mixed together.*"

But Tristan held Iseult, and a desire greater than mortal will worked in them, and he said:

"Well, then, let come Death!"

No sooner did he speak those words than the wind freshened, the sails filled, and the bark leaped through the foaming waves. All through the dark night, as the ship rolled beneath them and carried them racing toward the Cornish shore, they gave themselves up utterly to love.

5

Approaching the Wine

Tristan and Iseult drink the love potion, and in that instant romantic love enters our lives forever—for Tristan is Western man, and his life is our universal experience of romantic love. His wine-born rapture bespeaks a historical moment almost a thousand years ago when the cult of romance burst into our culture and started a slow evolution that spanned the centuries and formed our modern ideas about love.

We are about to approach the love potion in a new way. We have all tasted it, all been drunk on it; now we need to look at it consciously. This wine is heady and strong, and best approached with care; so we will pause here and try to form a clearer idea of what we mean when we speak of "romantic love."

In our culture people use this phrase, "romantic love," indiscriminately to refer to almost any attraction between man and woman. If a couple is having a sexual affair, people will say they are "romantically involved." If a man and a woman love each other and plan to marry, people will say it is a "romance," but in fact, their relationship may not be based on "romance" at all. It may be based simply on *love,* which is completely different from romance! Or a woman will say, "I wish my husband would be more romantic." But what she actually means is that her husband should be more attentive, more thoughtful, and show her more feeling. We are all so caught up in the belief that romantic love is "true love" that we use the term for many things that are not romantic love at all. We assume that if it is love, it must be "romance," and if it is romance, it must be "love."

The fact that we say "romance" when we mean "love" shows us that underneath our language there is a psychological muddle. Our confusion in language is the symptom that tells us we have lost the consciousness of what love is, what romance is, and what the differences are between them. We are confusing two great psychological systems within us, and this has a devastating effect on our lives and our relationships.

Most of us have known married couples who never went through the "romance" stage in their love. Perhaps they started as friends, knew each other a long time as ordinary people, and never experienced a romantic attachment. They simply loved each other and decided to make a life together. Or we have seen couples who started in a great flurry of romance but eventually graduated to the point where they accepted each other as ordinary human beings. They dropped their expectations of perfection and committed themselves to a human relationship rather than to a vision of romantic ecstasy.

It is hard for us to imagine that there could be any love, at least any worthwhile love, still alive for a couple after romance departs. But often these people have what the rest of us frequently lack: love, relatedness, stability, and commitment. In our culture we have romance in abundance: We fall in love, we fall out of love; we live through great dramas, filled with ecstasy when romance burns hot and filled with despair when romance grows cold. If we look at our own lives and at the people around us, we see that romance doesn't necessarily translate into love or relatedness or commitment. Romance is something distinct, something apart, a reality unto itself.

Here, then, is the starting point for our exploration: Romantic love is not *love* but a complex of attitudes *about* love—involuntary feelings, ideals, and reactions. Like Tristan, we drink of the potion and find ourselves possessed: caught in automatic reactions and intense feelings, a near-visionary state.

Our Western ideal of romantic love was born into our society in around the twelfth century—about the time that Tristan was drinking the love potion for the first time. At the beginning this cultural phenomenon was called *courtezia*—in English, "courtly love." Courtly love was based on a completely new view of love and relationship. Under the influence of certain religious ideas of that era, courtly love idealized a "spiritual" relationship between men and women. Courtly love was an antidote to the patriarchal attitude we see in Tristan's world: It idealized the feminine; it taught a rough knight like Tristan actually to worship the universal feminine, symbolized by the fair lady whom he served and adored. It is this worship that we see in Tristan as soon as he drinks the wine; we sense that it is not Iseult he sees but something divine embodied in her, something universal or transcendent that she symbolizes for him.

Under the laws of courtly love, each knight agreed to obey his lady in all things having to do with love, relationship, manners, and taste. Within her realm she was his mistress, his queen.

There were three characteristics of courtly love that will help us to understand it. First, the knight and his lady were never to be involved sexually with each other. Theirs was an idealized, spiritualized relationship, designed to lift them above the level of physical grossness, to cultivate refined feeling and spirituality. The second requirement of courtly love was that they not be married to each other. In fact, the lady was usually married to another nobleman. The knight-errant adored her, served her, and made her the focus of his spiritual aspiration and idealism, but he could not have an intimate relationship with her. To do so would be to treat her as an ordinary mortal woman, and courtly love required that he treat her as a divinity, as a symbol of the eternal feminine and of his feminine soul. The third requirement was that the courtly lovers keep themselves aflame with passion, that they suffer intense desire for each other, yet strive to spiritualize their desire by seeing each other as symbols of the divine archetypal world and by never reducing their passion to the ordinariness of sex or marriage.

The ideal of courtly love so caught the Western imagination that it became the driving force behind a flow of poetry, song, love stories, and plays. The French love stories were called *romans,* which was anglicized into "romance." In these romances were all the great themes that form the basis for our romantic literature. The knight sees a fair lady and is overwhelmed by her beauty and goodness; he worships her ever after as the embodiment of his inner ideal, his inner vision of the eternal feminine. Though filled with a holy passion for her, he never touches her, but he goes through great adventures and does mighty deeds to honor her, to live up to the sense of nobility that she inspires in him. For him she is not a woman; she is Blanchefleur, Iseult the Fair, Psyche, Beatrice, and Juliet—the archetypal feminine in her divine essence.

Our word *romantic* and our romantic ideal have come down to us through the romances. Romantic love is "story-book" love. But this is a story that all of us try to live out in our own ways within the down-to-earth world of human relationships and human practicality. Despite our sexual revolution, despite our modern tendency to sexualize every relationship, we still seek the same basic psychological patterns in our romances: a woman who is more than a woman, the symbol of something so perfect and divine that she inspires a passion that goes beyond physical attraction, beyond love, to a sense of worship. We seek the "spiritual" intensity, the ecstasy and the despair, the joyous meetings and the tearful partings, of the romances. And we also feel, like the knights of old, that all this uplifts us, refines us, and gives life a new and special meaning—a meaning we have lost with Blanchefleur's departure and a meaning we hope to find in Iseult the Fair.

We might expect that a cult of love that specifically opposes marriage, that encourages passionate relationships outside marriage, that seeks to spiritualize relationship into a perpetual and superhuman intensity, would be a very poor basis for marriage and a very risky approach to human relationships. Yet these are the ideals that underlie our patterns of courtship and marriage to this day! Taken on the wrong level, these inherited ideals cause us to seek passion and intensity for their own sake; they plant a perpetual discontent that can never find the perfection it seeks. This discontent grays over every modern relationship, holds an unattainable ideal before our eyes that blinds us perpetually to the delight and beauty of the here-and-now world.

There is something awesome in these huge, culturally transmitted systems of belief. One day we realize that we are completely possessed and dominated by a set of beliefs that we, as individuals, never chose. It is as though we breathed them in from novels and movies, from the psychological air around us, and they became part of us, as though fused with the cells of our bodies. We all know that we are supposed to "fall in love" and that our relationships must be based on romance—nothing less will do! Every man knows what he is supposed to feel in a relationship and what he is entitled to demand from his girlfriend or wife. It is all spelled out in detail in some unseen layer of his unconscious mind. This is "romance."

However, there is something real and true in romantic love, regardless of how we misunderstand it or misapply the ideal of our ancestors. There is a truth in the high tales of romantic love that thrills us. There is a truth in the noble deeds of the knight, the beauty and goodness of the lady, the sacrifices, the reverence, the quests, and the faithfulness unto death. In the aspirations of romantic love there is a deep psychological truth that reverberates in our souls, that awakens us to what we are at our best, what we are when we are whole. No one can hear these ancient romances and be unmoved, unless he be made of ice, for in these loves, adventures, and acts of devotion, there is revealed all that is noble, loving, faithful, and most high within our own selves.

If we must look at what has gone wrong with romantic love, let us also see what is right about it. In its purest form it is an ideal of great power, and contained within every such ideal is profound reality. They are not only ideals, they are windows on our souls that tell of a practical and living reality within us, something we can live and be. We may misunderstand the truth behind the ideal; we may try to live it on the wrong level or to put it in the wrong place; but the truth is there to enrich us and move us closer to wholeness. Our task is to find the truth in romantic love and the level on which this truth can live.

It is difficult to look objectively at romance; it is painful, for we fear that reality will drive out love, and that life will then be cold and dismal. But one of the great needs of modern people is to learn the difference between human love as a basis for relationship, and romantic love as an inner ideal, a path to the inner world. Love does not suffer by being freed from the belief systems of romantic love. Love's status will only improve as love is distinguished from romance.

Jung once quoted a medieval alchemist who said, "Only what is separated may be properly joined." When two things are muddled together they need to be separated, distinguished, and untangled so that they may later be rejoined in a workable synthesis. This is the correct meaning of "analysis" in psychology; to analyze is to separate out the entangled threads of one's inner life—the confused values, ideals, loyalties, and feelings—so that they may be synthesized in a new way. We analyze romantic love, not to destroy it, but to understand what it is and where it belongs in our lives. Analysis must always serve synthesis in order to serve life; what is taken apart must be put back together again.

The sorceress Queen has mixed strange and wondrous ingredients in her potion. There are secret herbs, magical spells, and unearthly powers. Brangien even says that the Queen mixed, "not love alone, but love and death together." We have all tasted of this brew and wandered into another world, drunk with magic. We have all been lovers, but now we can be alchemists: We will unmix the wine, we will distill out the herbs and spells. Then we will see what awesome forces are mixed in us, revealed in our capacity for both human and divine love.

6

The Wine of Herbs

Siempre fuiste la razon de mi existir
Adorarte para mi fué religion . . .

Es la historia de un amor
Como no hay otro igual,
Que me hizo comprender
Todo el bien, todo el mal;
Que le dió luz a mi vida—
Apagandola después . . .
Ay! Qué vida tan oscura!
Sin tu amor no vivire.

Always you were the reason for my existence;
To adore you for me was religion . . .

It is the story of a love
Like unto which there is no equal,
Which made me understand
All that is good, all that is bad;
That gave light to my life,
Extinguishing it afterwards . . .
Oh! What a darkened life!
Without your love I will not live.

Carlos Almarán, "Historia de un amor"

Before he drinks the potion, Tristan is just a knight who thinks he has done his duty to his king. He hunted the faraway princess and captured her, and he is carrying her home to the King. He expects to be even more famous, even more admired. But after a drink of this strange wine, Tristan stares into Iseult's eyes like one "ravished and apart." His whole world is turned upside down; he is stood on his head; all of his values are turned around. Until now he had been loyal to his king, but now, suddenly, all sense of duty is incinerated in the heat of his passion. Before, his great ambition was to be a renowned knight of Cornwall. Now, he is ready to trade everything, even life itself, for one night in Iseult's arms. He hears Brangien's warning: "This way lies death!" But his mind and tongue are enslaved to passion and he can only reply, "Well, then come Death."

What of Iseult? Before she drank the potion she hated Tristan. He was not only the murderer of her uncle, but the assassin of her pride, for he conquered her, won her heart, and then betrayed her. Now, with that wine coursing through her veins, she says, "You know that you are my lord and my master, and I your slave."

Although this scene is familiar to us, although we have experienced it in our own lives, yet there is something strange in it. Tristan and Iseult are "in love," yet we wonder if it is with each other. They are entranced, mesmerized, in love with a mystical vision—but of something separate and distinct from their human selves, something they see through the magic of the wine. Their "love" is not ordinary human love that comes by knowing each other as individuals. The symbol tells us that this is a love that is "magical," "supernatural"—it is neither personal nor voluntary; it comes from outside the lovers and possesses them against their will. It reminds us of what people often say: "They are in love with love."

The myth says that romantic love has the same qualities as the love potion. But the love potion is both natural and "supernatural." Partly it is wine and herbs from the earth, symbolizing the ordinary human side of romantic love. But partly it is magic spells and sorcery. What is it in romantic love that is evoked by these symbols?

We know there is something inexplicable in romance. When we look at the feelings that rampage through us, we know that it is not just companionship or sexual attraction, and it is not that quiet, devoted, unromantic love that we often see in stable marriages and relationships. It is something more, something different.

When we are "in love" we feel completed, as though a missing part of ourselves had been returned to us; we feel uplifted, as though we were suddenly raised above the level of the ordinary world. Life has an intensity, a glory, an ecstasy and transcendence.

We seek in romantic love to be possessed by our love, to soar to the heights, to find ultimate meaning and fulfillment in our beloved. We seek the feeling of wholeness.

If we ask where else we have looked for these things, there is a startling and troubling answer: *religious experience.* When we look for something greater than our egos, when we seek a vision of perfection, a sense of inner wholeness and unity, when we strive to rise above the smallness and partialness of personal life to something extraordinary and limitless, this is spiritual aspiration.

Here we are confronted with a paradox that baffles us, yet we should not be surprised to discover that romantic love is connected with spiritual aspiration—even with our religious instinct—for we already know that courtly love, at its very beginning so many centuries ago, was conceived of as a spiritual love, a way of loving that spiritualized a knight and his lady, and raised them above the ordinary and the gross to an experience of another world, an experience of soul and spirit. Romantic love began as a path of spiritual aspiration; unconsciously, we seek that same path in romantic love today.

In the symbolism of the love potion we are face to face suddenly with the greatest paradox and the deepest mystery in our modern Western lives: What we seek constantly in romantic love is not human love or human relationship alone; we also seek a religious experience, a vision of wholeness. Here is the meaning of the magic, the sorcery, the supernatural in the love potion. There is another world that is outside the vision of our ego-minds: It is the realm of psyche, the realm of the unconscious. It is there that our souls and our spirits live, for unknown to our conscious Western minds, our souls and spirits are psychological realities, and they live on in our psyches without our knowledge. And it is there, in the unconscious, that God lives, whoever God may be for us as individuals. Everything that resides on the other side, in the realm of the unconscious, appears to the ego as being outside the natural human realm; thus it is magical, it is supernatural. To the ego the experience of that other world is no different from religious experience; the religious urge, the aspiration, means a seeking after the totality of one's life, the totality of self, that which lives outside the ego's world in the unconscious in the unseen vastness of psyche and symbol.

This is the meaning of these symbols in our story, and this is the secret key that unlocks the mystery of romantic love.

Let us go back to Tristan's bark; here is Tristan, all aflame with wine. What is this fervor in his eyes? Iseult stands nearby him, but his eyes are focused on something distant—they are focused on infinity! He sees, not Iseult, but a vision. What is this trembling in his limbs? If we go to the cell of Saint John of the Cross, we will find this same look, this same staring in mystical contemplation. If we are transported across the sea to a temple in India, we will find a holy man trembling in the same ecstasy before an altar of Shiva. It is the same instinct, it is the same intense fervor, and it leads toward the same end: transcendence.

Romantic love has always been inextricably tied to spiritual aspiration. This is so obvious that it would seem unnecessary to say it, yet we all avert our gaze and miss the obvious. It is a truth too close to see. We only need to look at the love stories, the poetry, the songs that come from our romantic era, and we find that man-in-love has made of woman a symbol of something universal, something inward, eternal, and transcendent. What he sees in woman makes him feel that he has finally realized himself, that he sees all the meaning of life. He sees a special reality revealed in her; he feels completed, ennobled, refined, spiritualized, uplifted, transformed into a new, better, and whole man.

The great romantic poets do not hide this fact; they proclaim it. The troubadours and knights of Tristan's day proclaimed it openly. Unlike us, who think ourselves so sophisticated, they were fully conscious of what they sought through romantic love. They chose to give up seeing woman as woman and instead made her into a symbol of the eternal feminine, the soul, divine love, spiritual ennoblement, and wholeness. We may dispute whether this is the right vision of woman, whether it ennobles woman or demeans her to be made into a symbol of something other than what she is, to be made an ikon through which romantic man meditates on his vision of the eternal. But at this point, we just need to see that it is so.

In the Mexican love song quoted at the beginning of this chapter, we find all this condensed into a few lines. In the forthrightness of naive poetry the singer tells us what we don't often acknowledge: "Always you were the reason for my existence; To adore you for me was religion." When a human being becomes the object of this adoration, when the beloved has the power to "give light to our lives" or extinguish that light, then we have adopted the beloved as the image and symbol of God.

This is the most simple and direct description of what romantic love is. The reality that hides in romantic love is the fact of spiritual aspiration; the truth that the Western man unconsciously and involuntarily seeks in romantic love is the inner truth of his own soul. The Western man, without realizing it, is caught in a quest for wholeness and, against his wish, is pulled inexorably by a vision of the universal and the eternal. But it is in the image of woman, seen through the lens of romantic love, that he invests his quest and his vision.

Why is it that modern men won't admit what earlier men openly proclaimed and even idealized? It is because we won't consciously give a place to spiritual aspiration in our modern lives. It is out of fashion, we don't understand what it is, and we won't admit to it. We aren't consciously interested in wholeness—only in production, control, and power; we don't believe in the spirit—only in what is physical and sexual. But our urge toward the soul finds its way involuntarily into the one place we would never look for it—into the projections, the ideals, the ecstasies and despairs, the passions and strivings, of romantic love. For lack of any other channel, any other form in which it could be lived in our modern culture, our religious instinct has migrated almost completely into the one secret place where it is allowed to live *sub rosa:* romantic love. This is why we feel that our lives are absolutely meaningless except when we are "in love," and that is why romantic love has become the single greatest psychological force in our culture.

Myths are filled with paradox because reality is inherently paradoxical. In Greek, *paradox* means literally "against opinion"; that is, a paradox rubs against our accepted notions of reality. We like to believe that we already know everything, that we have everything figured out; this is why true paradox is always painful. Paradox conflicts with our prejudices, challenges our assumptions, and flies in the face of our collective "truths." This is why we prefer to call myths "fairy tales" and to relegate them to children. This is why we like to explain myths as fanciful inventions of primitive and childlike minds. If we take myths seriously as the statements of reality that they are, then we find all our comfortable platitudes, all our fixed notions of "truth," called disturbingly into question.

To look at a myth for wisdom is to return to the primal material of the psyche. All symbols in dreams and myths should strike us as paradoxical, for their whole purpose and their psychological role is to cut through the "known," and teach us something new from the unconscious. Whenever we find ourselves interpreting a dream or myth as confirmation of our ingrained opinions, then we are in trouble. Symbols do not flow from the unconscious to tell us what we already know but to show us what we have yet to learn.

So it is with the love potion. How much easier it would be to explain it as a fanciful superstition of the primitive twelfth-century mind! The love potion is the penultimate paradox! Nothing would go against opinion more than this—that it is our own religious instinct, our own unconscious quest for the "other world" that gives romantic love its magic, its unearthly intensity and otherworldly expectations. Nothing could violate our common sense more.

We assume we know what romantic love is, although we know nothing; we assume that we understand it perfectly, although in fact it is incomprehensible; we assume that we are controlling it, when in fact it possesses us. Our culture serves up a whole set of truths about romance that we unconsciously and automatically accept. We never question them, and we are irritated if anyone else does. But here we are confronted with the paradox, and we can't sidestep it: romantic love attempts to experience the "other world" in a searing, all-enveloping ecstasy that completes one—makes one feel psychologically whole, utterly fulfilled, and in touch with the meaning of life.

If we are mystified by this, that is exactly the point; romantic love is a mystery. It is an energy system that surges out of the unknown and uncharted depths of the unconscious, out of a part of ourselves that we don't see, don't understand, and can't reduce to common sense. Like the love potion, it seizes us against our will, stands us on our heads, turns our lives upside down, rearranges our loyalties. We forget our precious plans, give up our beliefs, and abandon the ways of life to which we have clung.

It is this out-of-control quality in romantic love that gives us the deepest clue to its real nature. This overwhelming, ecstatic "falling in love" with someone is an event, deep in the unconscious psyche, that happens *to* one. One does not "do" it, one does not control it, one does not understand it: It just happens to one.

This is why the Western male ego has such trouble coping with romantic love: It is, by definition, "out of control." It is out of control because that is what we secretly and unconsciously want from it—to be ecstatic, lifted out of the sterile confines of our tight little ego worlds.

That bursting of bonds, that transcending of the ego-mind, is "religious experience," and that is what we seek. Western men are taught that the male ego must have control over everything within and everything around it. The one power left in life that destroys our illusion of "control," that forces a man to see that there is something beyond his understanding and his control, is romantic love. Formal religion and the church have long since ceased to threaten Western man's illusion of control. He either reduces his religion to platitudes or ignores it altogether. He seeks his soul neither in religion nor in spiritual experience nor in his inner life; but he looks for that transcendence, that mystery, that revelation, in woman. He *will* fall in love.

We take a jaundiced view of religion in our age, partly because what passes for religion has ceased to have much meaning for many of us. Carl Jung opens up an approach that takes us back to the roots of religion—the experience of psyche as soul, as a reality. He discovered that each person's psychological structure includes an independent "religious" function. This does not mean there is a need necessarily to follow a particular creed or dogma. But it means that each human being comes with an inborn psychological urge to find a meaning in life. We all have an intuition that we could see ourselves as whole persons, see the ultimate meaning of life, experience ourselves totally. Jung saw that most Westerners, although they consciously only believe in what is physical and rational, have dreams and fantasies overflowing with symbols of those very qualities that people used to seek in their religious life: symbols evoking a sense of wholeness and a vision of a world larger than the ego.

We can look at the geography of the psyche and understand the religious side of life in a new way; it is the same religious faculty but approached with a different language. We see that this ego, this so-called conscious mind, is like an island in a vast ocean of psyche. Out there, in that ocean of being, outside the limits of the ego's world and beyond what it knows or can see, are the missing parts of our total selves. We are psychological beings: The greater portion of our totality is not physical, but psyche, and most of that is in the unconscious. Contrary to our popular notions of psychology, the unknown and unconscious parts of our totality greatly exceed the conscious parts. We do not find our sense of meaning, wholeness, or fulfillment within this tiny ego world. We sense that there is more, much more, out there, although we know neither where to look nor what we search for.

That which we seek manifests as a symbol; it surges out of the deep layers of the psyche as what was anciently named the *imago dei:* the god-image. The god-image flows out of psyche, manifesting our deep-rooted urge toward wholeness and unity. This spontaneously rising image, the imprint of what we seek, is the root source of our intuition that there must be something higher than this ego that pulls together all of life and all of phenomena, and that reveals to us the meaning of life. It creates in us a sense that the unitive vision is possible.

Jung tells us that our need to explore the far reaches of our own unconscious and our need for a religious life are the same need. This was well known in olden times:

> "For knowledge of man is the beginning of wholeness, but knowledge of God is perfect wholeness." Clement of Alexandria says in the *Paedagogus:* "Therefore, as it seems, it is the greatest of all disciplines to know oneself; for when a man knows himself, he knows God." And Monoimos, in his letter to Theophrastus, writes: "Seek Him from out of thyself and learn who it is that taketh possession of everything in thee, saying: *my* god, *my* spirit, *my* understanding,

> *my* soul, *my* body; and learn whence is sorrow and joy, and love and hate . . . and getting angry though one would not, and falling in love though one would not. And, if thou shouldst closely investigate these things, thou wilt find Him in thyself, the one and the Many." (Jung, *Aion,* p. 222 [paren. omitted]*)

In former times Western people experienced the god-image through their religion, through mystical contemplation, in ritual that still carried symbolic power for them, in the image of the historical church, the revealed Word, the saints, the community of believers. But in recent times many have lost the traditional vessels of the *imago dei.* If we ask ourselves why, we already have part of the answer in the story of Tristan: The patriarchal mentality of our society is inherently partial, dedicated to living the masculine side of human nature at the expense of the feminine and at the expense of wholeness. Into that tightly insulated mind, almost nothing can enter. We are proof against the unconscious, against feeling, against the feminine and against our own souls. The one place where we are vulnerable, the one place where our souls can break through our modern armor, is in our loves.

The meaning of the love potion is that the supernatural world suddenly invades the natural world through romantic love. The fire descends from heaven! The world of soul and spirit, the overwhelming power of the religious potentiality in the psyche, suddenly invades the ordinary world of human relationships. What we had always longed for, a vision of ultimate meaning and unity, is suddenly revealed to us in the form of another human being.

It is a momentous discovery that we have taken our instinct for wholeness and projected it completely into

---

*All such references to other works are given in short form in text. For full references, see the Bibliography.

our loves. We have taken the *imago dei* out of the temple, out of heaven, and suddenly relocated it here in our midst, contained in the relationship between two human beings. This is the incredible reversal of human instincts, the momentous rechanneling of human energies, that was accomplished in the sorcery of the love potion. In the feeling of being possessed by our loves, of being caught up in some power that completely overwhelms us, we rediscover our religious life. So long as we are "in love" with someone, the world takes on a brightness and meaningfulness that no mortal human being could ever bestow. But when we fall "out of love" the world suddenly seems dismal and empty, even though we are still with the same human being who had inspired such rapture before.

This is why men and women put such impossible demands on each other in their relationships: We actually believe unconsciously that this mortal human being has the responsibility for making our lives whole, keeping us happy, making our lives meaningful, intense, and ecstatic!

Someone once said, "The beginning of wisdom is a firm grasp of the obvious." If we will stop sipping the love potion long enough to look at it as symbol, perhaps it will awaken us to what is plain to see. As we continue our mythical journey with Tristan and Iseult, we will live with them the story of all lovers who have ever drunk the magic wine. We will see with greater clarity how we have mixed our spiritual aspiration—our urge toward the divine—with our human relationships. This is the secret knowledge that is hidden behind the mystery of romantic love: how to live with and honor both of these powerful energies, which we have mixed together so deliciously and yet so dangerously in the wine of love.

7

Iseult the Fair

In our journey we meet many aspects of the inner feminine and discover the role each has to play both in a man's psychology and in the dynamics of romantic love. We have met Blanchefleur, who symbolizes the fate of the feminine in our patriarchal world. Now comes Iseult the Fair, the most powerful and ubiquitous feminine presence in our modern world—and, perhaps for that very reason, the most difficult of all to comprehend.

Princess of the mystical isle, daughter of a sorceress Queen, skilled in the mysteries of magic and spirit, Iseult is part sorceress and part ordinary woman, part human and part divine. She is the inner ideal of the eternal feminine, the goddess who lives within a man's psyche, an image of beauty and perfection that inspires him to a sense of meaning in life.

Carl Jung had a special name for this aspect of our psyche; he called it *anima.* Anima literally means "soul" in Latin, for Jung discovered that anima personifies that part of the psyche that we have always called the "soul." Iseult the Fair appears constantly in the dreams and myths of men, often as a figure of superhuman beauty and divine significance. This is the part of himself that Tristan sees in Iseult in the moment after he drinks of the potion. A man feels that in her he will find the meaning of his life, find completeness, wholeness, and ecstatic experience.

The feminine principle within a man is above all a principle of relatedness; but anima delivers a man over to a special kind of relatedness: She personifies a man's capacity to relate to his own inner self, to the interior realm of his own psyche and to the unconscious. Curiously, she pulls him away from human relatedness, just as she pulls Tristan away from his human loyalty to his uncle and from his sense of duty and obligation. At a certain level of our evolution, our relatedness to our soul and our relatedness to our human, personal world are in deadly conflict—and this conflict is the crucible of consciousness.

Women have an equivalent psychological structure within, which Jung called "animus." Animus is the soul in woman just as anima is the soul in man. Animus usually personifies himself as a masculine force and appears in women's dreams as a masculine figure. Women relate to their animus side differently than men relate to anima, but there is one thing that men and women have in common: Romantic love always consists in the projection of the soul-image. When a woman falls in love it is animus that she sees projected onto the mortal man before her. When a man drinks of the love potion, it is anima, his soul, that he sees superimposed on a woman.

> The projection can only be dissolved when the son sees that in the realm of his psyche there is an imago . . . of the daughter, the sister, the beloved, the heavenly goddess, and chthonic Baubo. Every mother and every beloved is forced to become the carrier and embodiment of this omnipresent and ageless image, which corresponds to the deepest reality in a man. It belongs to him, this perilous image of Woman; she stands for the loyalty which in the interests of life he must sometimes forgo; she is the much needed compensation for the risks, struggle, sacrifices, that all end in disappointment; she is the solace for all the bitterness of life. And, at the same time she is the great illusionist, the

> seductress, who draws him into life with her Maya—and not only into life's reasonable and useful aspects, but into its frightful paradoxes and ambivalences where good and evil, success and ruin, hope and despair, counterbalance each other. Because she is his greatest danger she demands from a man his greatest, and if he has it in him she will receive it.
>
> This image is "My Lady Soul." (Jung, *Aion*, par. 24)

One of the peculiar developments in our Western world is that we no longer have any sense of having a soul. If we are asked what the soul is, our minds go blank. The word *soul* calls up neither feeling nor image; there is nothing in our feelings or our lives of which we can say, "That is my soul—there she is." It is a word that philosophers, theologians, and poets use, but we don't know why, and we secretly doubt that they know, either. "Soul" has become a mere figure of speech, a sentimentality.

Jung's psychology leads us back to soul as a concrete reality, capable of being known, described, and experienced with immediacy. Here is the point of intersection between the inner life that was found in the religions of old and the inner life of archetypal psychology; both attest the reality of the soul, and both know that it is only through the soul that we find the unconscious, the inner life, the side that is beyond ego and outside the narrow ambit of its peripheral vision.

There are three things Jung said of Soul that can guide us as we make this journey with Tristan and Iseult. First, the soul is not a figure of speech or a superstition: The soul is a psychological reality, an organ of the psyche; it lives on our unconscious side, but it affects our lives profoundly. Our soul is that part of the unconscious that is outside the ego, out of sight, yet mediates the unconscious to the ego. Dr. Jung said that the soul is "both receiver and transmitter," the organ that receives the images of the unconscious and transmits them to the conscious ego-mind.

Second, soul manifests itself, and the unconscious, by means of symbols: the images that flow from the unconscious in the form of dream, vision, fantasy, and all forms of imagination. The vital thing that Jung has discovered for us is that we have lost our sense of soul because we have lost our respect for symbols; our modern mind is trained that symbols are illusion. We say, "It is only your imagination," not realizing that all the missing parts of ourselves that we long for, the "lost lane into heaven," are constantly mediated to us in the forgotten language of the soul: the symbols and images that emanate through dream and imagination.

Third, for men, the symbol of soul is the image of woman. If a man is aware of this and knows when he is using the image of woman as the symbol of his own soul, then he can learn to relate to that image as symbol and to live his soul inwardly. Jung says, "It belongs to him, this perilous image of woman." When a man understands that this image is his, that it "belongs to *him*," then he has taken the first step toward consciousness in romantic love. He begins to see that "every beloved is forced to become the carrier and embodiment of this omnipresent and ageless image."

Each man must learn to relate to external people and situations. But it is equally important, and even more urgent, that he learn to relate to his own self. Until he learns to confront the motives, desires, and unlived possibilities of his own secret heart, he can never be complete within or genuinely fulfilled. That power within, which constantly urges us to experience our unlived possibilities and values, is the most awesome force in human life. Anima is that force for men: She is the soul. No wonder, then, that men see her as a goddess, she who alone can make their lives worth living! For ultimate meaning must be found within: A man must relate to the outer world from the strength of inner wholeness, not search aimlessly outside for a meaning that he finds, at last, only in the solitary pathways of his own soul.

Here we begin to understand part of what happens to Tristan when he drinks the love potion, and what he suddenly sees revealed in Iseult the Fair. As the magical wine inflames his limbs, he looks through new eyes. He sees not so much Iseult the woman, seated before him, but a radiant vision of the goddess within himself who is suddenly and magically in residence within the flesh of a mortal woman. He sees in Iseult his "Lady Soul," for Iseult has become her flesh, her image, and her symbol.

The beautiful and fine side of romantic love inheres in the truth of what is projected, in what is seen via one's beloved: soul, and its magical world of images. Who would deny this vision or this experience to a man or woman? Yet . . . there is another side, and we must face it. We look at Tristan: He has only just drunk the love potion, and what has happened? The ramifications in his human, practical world are terrible! He casts aside his duty to King Mark. He forgets his obligations. He gives up morality, loyalty, even necessity. The path of treason on which the lovers have set out can only lead to their destruction. He knows this, but it no longer matters: "Well then, come Death!"

In modern Westerners we see a host of complications that issue forth from this invasion of soul into the outer world, into our human relationships. A man actually begins to demand of his wife or girlfriend that she be the goddess, that she be his soul and bring him a constant, ecstatic sense of perfection. Rather than look within himself, where anima natively dwells, he demands his soul of his external environment; he demands it of woman. He is usually so busy projecting his inner ideal out onto her that he rarely sees the value and the beauty of the woman who is actually there. And if his projection suddenly evaporates and he is no longer "in love" in the romantic sense, then he finds himself in a terrible conflict. He wants to follow his projection as it flies off and alights on another woman, like a butterfly that moves from flower to flower. Here is the terrible conflict of values, the terrible conflict of loyalties that we see in Tristan: Suddenly our human loyalties and our soul-projections are going in different directions, absolutely at war within the delicate, easily cracked vessel of human relationship.

But behind all this clash of values there is something good, something fine, something of great evolutional power:

> The power that forces you into consciousness and that sustains you in your conscious world proves to be the worst enemy when you come to the next center, for there you are really going out of this world and everything that makes you cling to it is your worst enemy. The greatest blessing in this world is the greatest curse in the next. (Jung, "Kundalini Yoga," *Spring* 1976, p. 10–11

Whenever you are called by fate, whenever you are moved toward the next *chakra* (level of consciousness), there is a feeling of being "set on your head," of having your world turned upside down and finding that all the values and loyalties of the world you knew are in terrible conflict with the new world that calls to you.

Thus it is with romantic love: Patriarchal Western man has lost his soul, and his soul calls him forcibly, pulling him out his known world and into a realm where all seems upside down; and always, floating before his eyes, is the image of Iseult the Fair.

8

The Love Potion in History

Often the outside world seems to answer back to our inner journey: External life and history confirm what mythical symbols and dreams have taught us. From the love potion we have learned some startling things about the nature of this cultural and psychological phenomenon we call romantic love. We have also found that romantic love, in its origins as courtly love, was conceived as a "spiritual" discipline; this serves to confirm what the love potion symbolically implies. Now it will serve us to go back even further and to dig a little deeper; we will learn that the cult of courtly love had it roots in a religion.

For many centuries after the advent of the Christian era, Europe was a veritable marketplace of religions. As Christianity was imposed on various peoples by kings and emperors, they continued to worship, openly or secretly, their old gods and goddesses. People mixed their "pagan" religious practices with the veneer of Christian worship in combinations that would seem very strange to us today. Many of our secular holidays, such as May Day and Halloween, were originally religious celebrations; they are secular remnants of old religions that were suppressed by Christianity. The same is true of ideals and beliefs. Many of the attitudes and beliefs of the old religions were suppressed superficially as heresy but live on in us and in our culture unconsciously. And they live on for a reason: They correspond to a psychological need and a psychological reality within human beings that are served neither by orthodoxy nor by the "official" viewpoints.

This is one valid way of looking at romantic love as a psychological force: It is the vehicle in which something is returned to us that was cast out of our culture and out of our lives long ago. Human nature is resourceful; we find a way, even unconsciously, to hang onto what we need.

One of the most powerful of the early religions was the Manichaean movement, named for the Persian prophet Manes. In Europe this religion became "Catharism," for the believers called themselves Cathars, meaning "pure." By the twelfth century entire towns and provinces in the south of France, though nominally Christian, practiced Catharism, and many of the nobility in the courts of Europe were Cathars. In France the movement was called the Albigensian heresy because the movement centered in the city of Albi in France.

One of their basic beliefs was that "true love" was not the ordinary human love between husband and wife but rather the worship of a feminine savior, a mediator between God and man, who waited in the sky to welcome the "pure" with a holy kiss and lead him or her into the Realm of Light. By contrast with this "pure" love, ordinary human sexuality and marriage were bestial and unspiritual. Cathars believed that the love of man for woman should be an earthly allegory of their spiritual love for the Queen of Heaven.

Many Christians saw Catharism as a reform movement, a reaction against the corruption and politics within the religious heirarchy. The patriarchal church of the Middle Ages, long out of touch with the feminine soul, had become materialistic and dogmatic; it offered a "revealed" set of laws and teachings—all very rational and masculine. It offered a collective experience of ritual and dogma in which ordinary people found no room for a personal experience of a living god. By contrast, the Cathars practiced an exemplary morality and offered an experience of God that was at once personal, individual, and lyrical. They returned the feminine to religion: They returned Iseult the Fair.

The Cathars believed in a world of absolute good and evil. Spirit is good, but this physical world is evil. Our souls are actually angels, divine fragments of God that wandered from heaven and were imprisoned here in terrestrial matter. That heroic angel within each of us strives toward a pure spiritual existence in heaven, but Venus, goddess of sensuality, holds us down in dark physical matter. In order to find salvation, Cathars strove to be "pure," to give up the temptations that Venus put in their path, to give up sexuality, to eat sparingly, to escape from the sensual appetites that trap us in this evil, painful world. Thus, the Cathars avoided marriage and sexuality.

The focus of worship was the feminine savior: a being of pure light arrayed all in white, awaiting us in heaven to guide us into the presence of God. Salvation for Cathars came only through physical death: leaving this body and rising to meet the Lady on high. But a Cathar man's preparation for liberation from the flesh was to see woman, not as wife, not as mortal companion or sexual partner, but as the image of the Savior—to adore her with passion, but always as symbol, always as a reminder of the "other world" of purity and light.

The pope declared Catharism a heresy and Saint Bernard of Clairvaux drove it underground by relentless crusades. But like every powerful idea that is driven underground, it reappeared in another form—a supposedly "secular" form. The teachings and ideals of the Cathars suddenly reappeared in the cult of courtly love, in the songs and poems of the troubadours and in the "romances." Some cultural historians believe that courtly love was a deliberate "secular" continuation of Catharism, that the knights and ladies who first practiced courtly love were Cathars continuing their religious practice under the guise of a secular cult of love. To outsiders it looked like a new and elegant way to make love, to woo and flatter pretty damsels, but for the insider who knew the "code," it was an allegorical practice of Catharist ideals.

The ideal of courtly love swept through the feudal courts of medieval Europe and began a revolution in our attitudes toward the feminine values of love, relationship, refined feeling, devotion, spiritual experience, and the pursuit of beauty. That revolution finally matured into what we call romanticism. It also revolutionized our attitudes toward women; but it left a strange split in our feelings. On the one hand, Western men began to look on woman as the embodiment of all that was pure, sacred, and whole; woman became the symbol of anima: "My Lady Soul." But on the other hand, still caught in the patriarchal mind, men continued to see woman as the carrier of "feminine" emotionalism, irrationality, softness, and weakness—all of which are more symptoms of a man's own feminine side than they are characteristics of women.

It still hasn't occurred to Western man to stop looking on woman as the symbol of something and to begin seeing her simply as a woman—as a human being. He is caught in the ambivalence he feels toward his own inner feminine, sometimes rushing toward it in search of his lost soul, sometimes disdaining it as a needless complication in his life, a "wrench in the gears" of his patriarchal machinery. This is the unhealed split within man that he projects onto outer woman, the war he fights at her expense.

A few things have changed since the days of courtly love. At the beginning, when it was still a spiritual ideal, courtly love did not permit sexuality or marriage between the lovers. They sensed that the otherworldly intensity of the adoration could not mix with personal relationship, marriage, and physical contact. By contrast, we *always* mix romance with sex and marriage. The main notion that has not changed over the centuries is this: our unconscious belief that "true love" must be a mutual religious adoration of such overwhelming intensity that we feel all of heaven and earth revealed in our love. But unlike our courtly ancestors, we try to mix that worship into our personal lives, along with sex, marriage, cooking breakfast, paying the bills, and raising children.

The courtly belief that true love can only exist outside marriage is still with us today, unconsciously affecting us more than we know. A man expects his wife to take care of the children, have food on the table, contribute to the family income, and back him up in the daily struggles of human life. But some other part of him wants her to be the incarnation of anima, the holy Lady in the sky who is always beautiful and perfect. He wonders how the pure and shining goddess whom he adored turned into this ordinary wife who seems utterly unreasonable. A woman sees her husband working, paying the bills, getting the car repaired, and defending his empires, living the ordinariness of life. She wonders what happened to the knight who adored and worshiped her when he was "courting" her, in the days when everything was so intense, so ecstatic, so blissful. The old unconscious belief returns to haunt them, whispering that "true love" is somewhere else, that it can't be found within the ordinariness of marriage.

These are the terrible splits that we all carry around within us. On one hand, we want stability and relationship with an ordinary human being; on the other hand, we unconsciously demand someone who will be the incarnation of soul, who will reveal the godhead and the Realm of Light, who will move us to a state of religious adoration and fill our lives with ecstasy. Here we find, still living within us, the Catharist fantasy, the religious ideal in disguise.

Each of these ideals is a psychological truth; each is a fantasy playing through us, telling us who we are, what we are made of, and what we need.

The religion of the Cathars and its offspring, courtly love, are carriers of the most magnificent fantasy in the mind of Western man, the fantasy that romantic love carries for us today. But this awesome fantasy is no illusion: All fantasy is reality, reality expressed in symbol and flowing from an ineffable source. Catharism is the fantasy of finding one's lost soul. It is the wondrous fantasy of discovering that the inner world is real, that the soul is real, that the gods are real, and that we can truly find that world, that beauty, that communion with the gods.

Many men would agree that romantic love is a "fantasy," but they would not know how great a thing they said —for as it is a fantasy, it is also a truth, a truth that we can live, if we will understand it on the right level. The truth behind fantasy has to be earned. To find that reality, we must look behind the fantasy and its symbols; we have to give up trying to live the Catharist and courtly fantasies literally—outside ourselves, with mortal people in the temporal world—and live this fantasy's truth as an inner event, an inner fact, experienced in the timeless realm of Her whom we now affirm.

9

Guile and Force

We have sailed with Tristan on two voyages over the seas to Ireland. The first time he is sick unto death; he floats on the water with only his harp, trusting in the sea to bring him to his cure. His inner journey brings him to Iseult the Fair, a woman of surpassing beauty and wondrous gifts, but curiously, there is no reaction. He is not interested in Iseult; if he loves her, he does not yet know it; he makes no effort to befriend her or win her over. He only wants her to heal him—then back to Cornwall, back to his status quo.

Back in Cornwall there are disturbing events and disturbing attitudes. King Mark does not want a queen. In all the many years since Blanchefleur died there has been no feminine presence in the court of Cornwall, yet King Mark does not want to marry; he wants neither wife nor queen. He hears, surely, of Iseult the Fair, but he shows no more interest than Tristan. The King and his nephew return to their norm; they content themselves with staging bloody jousting matches, winning wars, slaying enemies, killing dragons, and other such favorite masculine pastimes. And when Tristan does return to Ireland, it is not because he seeks Iseult for her own sake, not because he values her and what she represents, not because he wants to make a relationship with her. He goes like a raiding pirate, "by guile and by force," to carry her off as the spoils of battle.

Why does Tristan set off on his quest for the Queen of the Hair of Gold? At first his motives seem noble and brave: He says to King Mark, "I would put my life into peril for you, that your barons may know that I love you loyally." But behind these words we know what he is saying: He wants to use Iseult as a pawn in his competition with the barons; he wants to bring her home as a feather in his cap, a trophy to his manhood, proof that he is the most loyal and heroic of champions in the court of Cornwall. Thus it is that we turn the virtues of the hero into a vice, for in Tristan's attitude toward Iseult is reflected a Western man's attitude toward his soul.

When we are so wounded that nothing else will avail, when we can find nothing within the ego's bag of tricks that will restore meaning or sanity to our lives, then we will reluctantly go to our souls. Like Tristan, we will finally set ourselves adrift in the unconscious: We will finally explore our inner domains and look for the meaning of our lives. But once we have gone there and have found healing at the hands of Iseult, we instantly refocus on our patriarchal ego lives: our projects, our production lines, our status and prestige in the external world. Like Tristan, we become overconcerned with appearances: What do the other barons think of us? Who is the greatest champion of all? Who produces the most? Who makes the most money?

King Mark's refusal to marry is an ominous symbol. In myth or dream the king's failure to take a queen and produce an heir symbolizes a refusal of wholeness, a refusal to grow, a refusal of the destiny that comes in the form of the new child. In olden times people worried when the king had no children; they feared that the soil would not be fertile, that the rains would not fall, that their families would have few children, that the kingdom would go dry and sterile. By contrast, the marriage of the king or queen and the birth of an heir brought them joy. Even today, when a monarch or a prince produces a child, especially an heir to the throne, the whole world is interested and millions of people rejoice as though they were personally involved with the child. There is a deep psychological energy underlying our collective reaction to the birth of a royal child. At the deepest level of the psyche the King and Queen symbolize to us the evolution of the whole self, and the newborn heir symbolizes the new consciousness and power that we hold within ourselves in potential.

Whatever might be our conscious attitudes toward royalty, we will do well to remember that there is an archetypal royalty within each of us. The symbol of King and Queen points our consciousness toward what is highest and most true within us, and toward our potential for making a synthesis of masculine values with feminine values.

So King Mark's refusal to take a queen tells us that something is amiss in the Western male psyche: Not only has he lost the feminine, but he is not interested—he doesn't even consciously know that he has lost it. We have pursued our masculine and extroverted values for so long that we have come to see the soul as an unnecessary complication in an otherwise neat and tidy masculine world.

Strangely, it is the "felon" barons, Tristan's mortal enemies, who challenge this state of affairs. From Tristan's viewpoint they are the "bad men" in the psyche. But it is always something we look on as evil in ourselves that forces us toward wholeness. It is a threat, a fly-in-the-ointment, something that upsets our ego worlds and our production-line lives. It may be illness, exhaustion from overwork, a neurosis that suddenly wells up and disrupts our lives, forcing us to look for the meaning behind what we can't explain. Our symptoms and our complications appear to us as "felons" who only want to make trouble, but it is the felons who force us to look for the queen.

When we finally go to look for her, we go, like Tristan, with "guile and force." When our lives go sterile, we go looking for anima. But we want her on our own terms; we want to appropriate her as an appendage of our egos, an ornament of our personas. We want anima to energize us, spark our lives, give us a sense of meaning and direction, and make our lives more exciting; but we don't want to learn from her on her terms, and we don't want to treat her as an equal. Tristan wants to use Iseult as a pawn of statecraft, as a means of sealing alliances between male egos. This is our usual attitude.

Tristan, who tells us of our heroism, also shows us where our heroism goes astray. Tristan is in the bath of herbs when he convinces Iseult of his devotion with honeyed words:

> "King's daughter. . . . One day two swallows flew, and flew to Tintagel and bore one hair out of all your hairs of gold, and I thought they brought me good will and peace, so I came to find you over seas. . . . I braved the monster and his poison. See here, amid the threads of gold upon my coat your hair is sown: the threads are tarnished, but your bright hair still shines."

It may be that all the tragedy in modern man's life begins in this one fatal deception—for it is himself that he deceives. The beauty in Tristan's words is that they are so right; the tragedy in his words is that he does not mean them! If he meant them, it would represent a great evolution, a reversal in the Western male ego, an affirmative seeking after the feminine. But if our patriarchal ancestor Tristan did not mean what he said, what about us? Could we learn to approach the feminine side of life with these same fine words and mean them? Anima sends us tidings of peace. After centuries of guile, can we learn to approach her honestly?

When Iseult hears Tristan's fine words, when she hears that one of her own golden hairs is sewn into his coat of arms, she lowers the sword. She goes to find the proof of his devotion, and thinking she has found it, she puts the sword away. Instead of stabbing him, she kisses him. Here we see a way in which inner feminine and outer woman are alike. The dominant principle for each is relatedness.

Like Iseult, if a woman is ignored or hurt by a man, she will often find a way to turn his own sword against him, to wound him through his own power drive. But in the instant that a man wakes up to his own need, offers his love, and affirmatively relates to her, woman has an almost magical power to forgive. The feminine makes use of the sword of her antagonist; when he buries his sword and offers relatedness, she buries her sword in the same instant. Aggression is transformed into relatedness. The feminine, whether in a woman or a man, will usually drop her grudges, and forget the wounds of the past if she is offered genuine relatedness and affection in the present. This is one of the most noble and beautiful instincts in woman, one of the ways that she serves and transforms life. Relatedness is her first principle, the dominant theme of her nature, that for which, more than all else, she lives.

So it is with Iseult. When Tristan convinces her that he offers relatedness and love, that he values her and desires her in her own right, then all her hatred and plans of revenge are set aside; she lowers the sword. Here are two sides of anima. The soul is not just some warm sentiment that we carry around in us to be taken out at need and otherwise ignored. She, too, requires relatedness—to one's inner world. She, too, requires something of a man's time and effort. When he ignores her, she rises in wrath. Anima comes charging with his own sword in hand and threatens to run him through. She upsets his life, creates obsessions and neuroses, and finds her way into the projections and upheavals of romantic love. Anima, with sword in hand, is a dangerous being, capable of leaving a trail of destruction in her path. But anima, like Iseult, will make peace. If we go in search of her, if we treat her as an equal, if we seek her world and her wisdom, she will make peace and she will open up to us her inner world.

Unfortunately, Western man is like Tristan: a smooth talker. But here is a riddle that offers redemption: Often when we lie we inadvertently speak the truth. What we think consciously we don't mean is exactly what is true on the unconscious level. Tristan believes that he lies. He does not know that, underneath his conscious motives, the unconscious draws him inexorably toward Iseult. And everything he has said to her is *true* in his deepest being, although he will be the last to realize it.

Why does Iseult believe him? The soul is a magic seer; she is no fool! Why does she believe him? Because she hears the truth beneath the lie, and it is to the deepest truth that the inner feminine responds.

Our deceits often express our deeper unconscious needs and desires, those that we will not consciously acknowledge. This principle does not give us license to deceive or to betray, but if we would learn to look for the truth underneath our deceptions, both when we find ourselves lying to ourselves and when we find ourselves lying to others, then we could begin to take responsibility for those truths and begin to live them directly and honestly.

Like Tristan, we have all spoken flowery words we thought we did not mean. But if we will look carefully to see from what secret and hidden place those words came, we will discover that it is Iseult that we seek and Iseult that we need.

Tristan does not know what it is that he seeks, nor what he needs, and so by a strange reverse alchemy of unconsciousness, he turns his truth into a lie. When Iseult stands before the Irish barons and hears the purpose of Tristan's quest and finds herself deceived, a knife pierces her heart, and she trembles "for shame and anguish."

> Thus Tristan, having won her, disdained her; the fine story of the hair of gold was but a lie! It was to another he was delivering her. . . . So . . . did Tristan by guile and by force conquer the Queen of the hair of gold.

But force and guile will never work in the end. By guile and force this male ego is pitted against its own self —against its innermost needs and against its own soul. Tristan believes he has conquered the feminine, that he will draw her home to serve alliances and male ego power. But he knows not what lies ahead of him. He thinks he has conquered, but it is he who will be conquered.

Fate sets before Tristan a cool clay pitcher filled with a rare and refreshing wine. And he, all unsuspecting, drinks deeply.

PART III

THE NARRATIVE

How Tristan and Iseult Wandered in the Enchanted Orchard

Now we return to our story, and we find Tristan and Iseult on a small ship headed for the coast of Cornwall. Tristan holds in his arms the Queen of the Hair of Gold —she who was meant for the King.

King Mark was amazed and all the people filled with delight when they saw their new Queen, for she was the fairest maiden ever seen in that land, and she was gracious alike to the noble and the lowly. The royal wedding was held amid splendor and rejoicing. But on the wedding night Iseult sent Brangien, her maid, to the bed of the King in her place. She arrayed Brangien in her fine clothes and put a magic spell over Brangien to deceive the King. Thus was the King fooled, and he never knew that his Queen had lost her maidenhood in the arms of his fair nephew before ever she set foot on the shores of Cornwall.

All the barons and the people were glad of the Queen. But in the hearts of Iseult and Tristan a fire flamed and would not be contained. Heedless of danger, they met in secret and took their fill of passion.

Behind the palace was a fine garden with fragrant flowers and a bubbling spring, and in the midst stood a tall pine-tree. Under that tall pine the lovers were wont to meet, shielded, so they thought, from all prying eyes.

And when they felt the sorrow of parting, at the trumpets of dawn, Iseult would sometimes say:

"Oh, Tristan, I have heard that the castle is fairy and that twice a year it vanishes away. So is it vanished now and this is that enchanted orchard of which the harpers sing. A wall of air girdles it on all sides; there are flowering trees, a balmy soil; here without vigil the hero lives in his friend's arms and no hostile force can shatter the wall of air." . . .

"No," said Tristan, . . . "this is not the enchanted orchard. But, one day, friend, we shall go together to a fortunate land from which none returns. There rises a castle of white marble; at each of its thousand windows burns a lighted candle; at each a minstrel plays and sings a melody without end; the sun does not shine there but none regrets his light: it is the happy land of the living."

Such were the glances that passed between them day by day that all their passion could be read by any who troubled to look. So those felon barons—whom God curse!—spied on them and betrayed them to the King. Taking the King to the trysting place, they lifted him into the pine-tree; and there he waited until he saw Iseult come stealing into the garden. But so bright was the moon that Iseult saw the shadow of the King on the ground. Then she trembled and prayed that Tristan would not come.

Soon Tristan leaped over the wall like a quiet panther, and Iseult cried, with stern tone of warning: "Sir Tristan, tell me quickly why you have asked to meet with me so secretly, for the King would think the worst if he knew, and it would be my life."

Then Tristan looked into the water of the spring and saw the King's reflection, and knew why Iseult spoke so sternly. Now Tristan's wits were as quick as his sword. He knelt and begged the Queen to be his intercessor with King Mark, to tell the King of his loyalty. He wept that false traitors had accused him and the Queen. And he said: "Know, oh Queen, that I will meet any knight in combat to prove your purity and my own innocence."

Thus did the lovers play act until King Mark thought them innocent, and he lowered the arrow he held drawn against the string, aimed at Tristan's heart.

Now, when Iseult told Brangien the night's adventure, Brangien cried: "Iseult, God has worked a miracle for you, for he is compassionate and will not hurt the innocent in heart."

But the King was filled with wrath at the four felon barons, and they fled from his sight.

Still Tristan would not give up the Queen, and he took every risk to hold her in his arms and take his fill of pleasure. Finally they were caught, and the proofs so plain that the King raged like a wounded boar and sent the lovers to the stake to be burned. But on his way to the stake, Tristan was led by a small chantry on the cliffs that overlooked the sea, and his guards let him enter to say his last prayers. Once in the chapel he said: "Rather will I jump from this cliff than go in shame to the stake!" And he threw himself through the window and over the cliff. But a strong wind caught his cloak, the breath of God slowed his fall, and he landed safe on the sands of the seashore. His faithful squire, seeing all that befell, dashed to the shore with horse and arms, and the two raced away.

The King, in burning wrath, gave Iseult to a band of lepers, to lie with her and take their pleasure, and so condemn her to a long and slow death. But Tristan burst upon the lepers with sword in hand and hewed them down and seized Iseult and so escaped with her into the wild Forest of Morois.

For three years the lovers lived in the wild wood.

They lived on roots and herbs and the flesh of wild animals. Their skin stretched tight over their thin bodies, they were pallid and their clothes were ragged. But they gazed at one another, and the potion coursed in their blood, and they did not know that they suffered.

One day, perchance, they happened on the hermit Ogrin, a holy and righteous man, who no sooner set eyes on Tristan than took him to task:

"*God aid you, Lord Tristan, for you have lost both this world and the next! A man that is traitor to his lord is worthy to be torn by horses and burnt upon the faggot, and wherever his ashes fall no grass shall grow. . . . Lord Tristan, give back the Queen to the man who espoused her lawfully according to the laws of Rome. . . . Do penance, Tristan.*"

But Tristan answered:

"*And of what crime should I repent, Ogrin, my Lord? . . . You that sit in judgment upon us here, do you know what cup it was we drank upon the high sea? That good, great draught inebriates us both. I would rather . . . live off roots and herbs with Iseult than, lacking her, be king of a wide kingdom.*"

Then said Iseult to Lord Ogrin:

"Sire, por Dieu omnipotent
Il ne m'aime pas, ne je lui.
Fors par un herbé
Dont je bui
Et il en but: ce fu pechiez."*

"Lord, by God Almighty,
He does not love me,
Nor I him.
It was because of an herb potion
Of which I drank
And he drank, too: it was a sin."

*Text in old French is taken from the Béroul version of the myth.

So did Tristan and Iseult disclaim their fault and tell Ogrin that the fault lay in the potion. And they withdrew from him back into the forest.

Soon after, a cunning woodsman found their hut in the woods, and running straightaway to Tintagel, this shameless traitor sold himself to the King to guide him there. When the King came nearby them, he dismounted and approached stealthily with sword in hand. But when he came upon the lovers they lay fully clothed, asleep on the ground, with Tristan's naked sword between them. And their faces were chaste and innocent.

Then the King said within himself:

"*My God, I may not kill them! For all the time they have lived together in this wood, had it been with a mad love that they loved each other, would they have placed this sword between them? Does not all the world know that a naked sword separating two bodies is the proof and the guardian of chastity? If they loved each other with a mad love, would they lie here so purely?*"

Then Mark took a ring from his hand and slipped it onto Iseult's finger, and taking Tristan's sword from the ground, he thrust his own sword in its place. So did he leave them signs of reconciliation and forgiveness.

Tristan and Iseult awoke of a start and found the King's ring and sword, and their sudden fear changed slowly to wonder. The King's compassion unsettled them as his hatred never could. For the first time, Tristan wondered if he did right; he longed for his uncle's love and comradeship.

"But," he thought, "he will take back Iseult! What am I thinking? How could I bear that? Better the King had killed me in my sleep, for now by his compassion he was awakened by conscience!"

Tristan thought how Iseult had been Queen by Mark's side, how she had lived in a palace hung with fine silks;

but in the woods she lived like a slave, wasted her youth in a savage life in a tiny hut.

"Indeed," he thought, "she is his wife. And she is Queen, wed by the laws of God and crowned before all the barony. Surely I must yield her to the King."

But all through the night he was undecided, and tortured with sorrows.

Iseult, in her turn, also had second thoughts:

"Tristan should have lived in the King's palace among his squires. He should have gone forth on adventures, but through me he has forgotten his knighthood and is hunted and exiled from the court, leading a random and wasted life!"

So Tristan and Iseult decided that she ought to return to the King.

But Tristan said:

"Queen, whatever may happen, and wherever I shall go, I shall be only yours, for I will serve only a single love."

Then the lovers set forth to the edge of the forest, to find Ogrin the Hermit. And instantly on seeing them he shouted:

"My friends, will you not at last come, and repent your madness? Tristan, my son, will you not yield back the Queen and seek the King's mercy?

And Tristan answered: "My lord, Ogrin, for our love there can be no penance. But I would not that Iseult languish here in this wretched land longer for my sake. Pray, my lord, send a writ to the King, and say that if he will take the Queen, I will return her. And if he will have me for his liege, so shall I return and do my duty as I ought."

Ogrin went before the altar and prayed and praised God. Then the good hermit made the writ and wrote in it fine words such as a priest would know, and sent it the same night to King Mark.

So soon as the King gathered his barons, who owed him counsel, he showed them the writ and ordered it read to them. And the barons said:

"King, let the Queen return and stay beside you. As for Tristan, let him leave this land and serve a king in France or, mayhap, the King of the Northlands. For, should he return to Tintagel, then will there be divers rumors and gossip and the crown be dishonored."

So it was. King Mark sent his message to Tristan to return the Queen at the river fords on a day certain, and to quit the land of Cornwall to serve in other lands.

On the day that Tristan returned Iseult, the lovers sat together in a fair place in the woods and wept sadly. And before they went to meet the King they made vows, one to another, in this wise:

"Queen," said Tristan, "Wherever my path may lead, I will send you messengers. And, should you ask, I shall come, no matter in what lord's service I ride, no matter how far away."

Iseult gave Tristan a green jasper ring, and said:

"*And friend, I have here a ring of green jasper. Take it for the love of me, and put it on your finger: then if anyone come saying he is from you, I will not trust him at all till he show me this ring, but once I have seen it, there is no power or royal ban that can prevent me from doing what you bid—wisdom or folly.*"

After Iseult returned, all the land was happy again, and all the Cornish people lived their lives in peace. But the felon barons still spoke evil of Iseult and said she had done evil with Tristan, and word came to her ears. So Iseult demanded of her husband and King that which was her right: the Trial of God. And this is the manner of that trial: An iron bar is heated until red hot; Iseult must swear the truth of what she says on the relics of the saints; then she must grasp that hot iron bar in her hands. If she speaks the truth, God will not let the iron burn her (as all good Christians know). But if she lies, then will it burn her, and on that evidence she must be burned at the stake for her treason.

Iseult sent word to Tristan for help in a secret plan. So it was that, on the day of the trial, Tristan came to the shore disguised as a poor pilgrim, all in rags. All was made ready for the trial: A hot fire burned, the saints' relics were nearby under guard, and the stake was ready with dry branches and kindling all around it.

The Queen came from the sea in her boat and, pointing at Tristan, she said to a knight:

"Fetch me that poor pilgrim to carry me across the mud, that I may come before the people clean and seemly."

Then Tristan waded into the shallows and lifted the Queen from the boat and carried her up to the dry land. Dressed in a snow-white robe she stood before all the barony of Tintagel and of Camelot—for even King Arthur and all his court came from Camelot to be witnesses, that none might ever question the judgment of God. And all stood astonished at her beauty. Then, holding the relics of the saints, she made her oath:

"I swear upon the saints that no man has ever held me in his arms except my husband the King and also that poor pilgrim who carried me from my boat."

Then the Queen, pale with fright but firm with good courage, went to the fire and picked up the red-hot iron. Holding it before her, she took nine slow steps, and then cast it upon the ground. Stretching her arms in the form of the cross, she faced the people and slowly opened her hands. And behold! the palms of her hands were cool and clean. The people stood silent, amazed, and then all at once broke into praise of God and wept with joy for their Queen.

Even after all these troubles and narrow escapes, Tristan would not leave Cornwall; nor could he keep himself from the Queen. Stealthily one night he went beneath her window and made the call of the nightingale. The Queen knew that call; she remembered her oath to God, her oath to Ogrin, her oath to the King; she felt the danger of death. Yet she cried:

"What does death matter? You call me, you want me, I come!"

And so they met in the darkness of the nights and took their fill of love. But treasonous spies and felons gathered around and spied on the Queen, and they knew they would soon be discovered again. Finally Tristan left, after many tearful words of parting, and quit himself of Cornwall.

Apart the lovers could neither live nor die, for it was life and death together; and Tristan fled his sorrow through seas and islands and many lands.

10

The Queen of the Inner World

When Iseult weds King Mark of Cornwall, it represents something deep and powerful in our psyche. Anima is returned to the inner kingdom; feminine and masculine are joined; the self is completed and made whole. We hear bells pealing; the people crowd into the great church and line the streets to behold the new Queen and rejoice in her beauty. The soul has returned to Cornwall; the King has a wife; the land bursts into bloom.

We should give pause to appreciate what this means to us; for there is a corresponding marriage within us, a union we should not hold lightly. Iseult has been the Queen from the moment that a sparrow flew through the window of Tintagel and brought her golden hair to Mark. Tristan calls her the Queen before she is married to King Mark and addresses her as "Queen" even in the wilds of Morois. Iseult the Fair is first, last, and always the Queen: She can be nothing else.

The royal marriage tells us that it is correct that anima should be joined to the inner King. Even though Tristan tricked her and used force and guile, even though his motives were wrong and she came against her will, even though they drank the love potion on the high seas, nevertheless, Iseult is the Queen of the inner world, and she is destined for only one place: to be Queen on the throne next to King Mark, the inner King. No other place can be appropriate to her royalty and her divinity.

If we see this, then we understand why Tristan destroys the kingdom when he betrays King Mark. Not only does he betray the King, he reduces the Queen to a place of lesser dignity than is her right. This not only affects Tristan in his personal world but affects the whole kingdom. When Iseult married King Mark, healing and joy flowed through the whole land. When Tristan beguiles Iseult into secret trysts beneath the pine-tree, the reverberations are felt everywhere: The Queen is made less than she is; she is toppled from her throne and is banished. The Queen's heart is divided; Tristan is divided; and soon the kingdom will be filled with discord because they can not resolve the conflict within themselves.

The dilemma of the myth, and the source of all the conflicts, confusions, and sufferings, is one simple demand: Tristan demands the right to possess Iseult for himself. She who should be Queen for a whole kingdom is stolen away by an individual. Ego usurps that which belongs to the self.

Now, what does this mean in the lives of modern men? The way that we pull anima away from her correct role within us, as Queen of the inner world, is by our attempts to make her into an external, physical woman. We do this by projection. This is our ego's way of trying to *possess* anima, to imprison her in mortal flesh, to experience her on a personal, external, physical level.

One specific thing is required in order to return anima to her psychological role as Queen of the inner world: A man must be willing to *withdraw the projection* of anima from the women in his life. This alone makes it possible for anima to perform her correct role within his psyche.

This alone makes it possible for him to see his woman as she is, unburdened by his projections.

Jung says this about the reclaiming of the projection:

> The withdrawal of the projections makes the anima what she originally was: an archetypal image which, in its right place, functions to the advantage of the individual . . . functioning between the ego and the Unconscious. . . . (Jung, *Psychology of the Transference,* par. 504*)

What is her "right place?" It is "functioning between the ego and the Unconscious," living in a man's inner psyche, his imagination, inspiring him from within.

When Tristan demands that he possess the Queen, it means that he insists on making anima into a physical being. He tries to make his soul physical, rather than recognize that she is a psychological being who lives in the inner world. Instead of experiencing her through symbol, as an inner feminine image, he tries to turn her into a literal physical woman. We not only take woman's image as the symbol of anima, but we forget that we have made her a symbol. We believe that anima is woman, and that woman is anima. We demand of women that they act out that role and be goddesses rather than human beings. By humanizing anima we lose sight of our souls; by trying to make women divine we lose sight of their humanity and rob them of their womanhood.

Iseult's royal marriage and her coronation as Queen tell us that she must always reign in the inner world as Queen. Try as we will, we may not draw her away from the inner King, pull her away from her royal marriage, or extrovert her into our physical relationships. If we try to do any of these, the kingdom is torn apart, the structure of human life and human relationships is damaged. And because Tristan keeps trying to see anima as physical

*For full quotation of this passage, see Chapter 16.

woman, he never experiences her as "My Lady Soul," which is his true desire and deepest wisdom.

There is another way. We can learn to differentiate the inner from the outer, relinquish the Queen to the King, and let her reveal a whole new world of consciousness—a world we can only see when we go to her as archetype, experienced within.

Tristan knows, in his deepest heart, that Iseult must always be the Queen. This is why he never tries to make an ordinary marriage with her; this is why, at a crucial moment, he places the naked sword between himself and Iseult. Ultimately, he knows he can not possess her in a personal and physical way. He relinquishes her to the King with one hand, even as he tries to possess her with the other. He does this unconsciously, begrudgingly, bemoaning his fate and not seeing the reasons behind his own actions.

If Tristan could make this sacrificial act consciously, if he could put the Queen back on her throne and understand why this must be so, his fate would not be the tragic story that it is. He could stay close by his Queen; he could experience her as the goddess that she is; he could live with her inwardly, on the correct level. He would have his soul, the High Queen, as inner reality, and he would be free to live with a mortal woman outwardly, to love her intensely *in her own right,* as is her due.

11

Deceit Beneath the Pine

And of what should I repent, Ogrin, my lord? . . . You that sit in judgment upon us here, do you know what cup it was we drank upon the high sea? That good, great draught inebriates us both.

With these words Tristan answers when Ogrin the Hermit calls him to repent of treason and adultery. And with these words, a new morality enters the world. Those who drink of the love potion claim a special dispensation. Tristan tells us he is innocent, that he has done no wrong, that he answers to a new set of laws. Inebriated as he is upon the magic wine, he is lifted above the old standards of right and wrong: He will not be judged by any rule save the law of passion. And God has intervened on his side so many times that he seems rightfully to claim the imprimatur of heaven.

The first time is beneath the tall pine-tree, the secret place where the lovers meet. The moon is in league with them and reveals that the King watches from on high in the tree. And when they have acted their roles and fooled the King, Brangien exclaims:

> "God has worked a miracle for you, for he is compassionate and will not hurt the innocent in heart."

What is this? Here is a contradiction difficult to explain. How are these lovers "innocent in heart" even as they betray the King, break their vows to him, and make a fool of him? Is this the same God who sanctifies marriage? who enjoins faithfulness and truth? Has God drunk the same wine as the lovers and begun to help in treasons and adulteries?

But there is more. When the lovers are caught, and Tristan is marched to the stake, he jumps off a cliff. Miraculously, a sudden and powerful wind billows out his cloak, which has caught on his boot, and breaks his fall. Later, when King Mark comes upon the lovers lying together in the wood of Morois, it happens that Tristan has put his naked sword between himself and Iseult; the lovers are saved again. Finally, when Iseult stands before all the assembled barony to endure the Judgment of God, she lifts up a red-hot bar and she is not burned. God himself confirms that she speaks "truth."

What are these miracles? What can they mean? They are not mere dramatic devices. If we can understand it, the lovers speak truly: They are "the innocent"! They are "the pure in heart." They have been overcome by a truth and a power so awesome that they have lost their bearings; they resonate to another world, to a different level of existence, and it has set them in opposition to all the standards of the ordinary human world.

These miracles tell us that the lovers do right even as they seem to do "wrong." At least, they do the best they can with the terrible revelation that has fallen on them. The "other world" intervenes over and over into ordinary life to relieve the two lovers of the normal consequences of their acts, for if they are out of step with this ordinary world and with human morality, they are completely *in* step with that other world. But that world exacts its own prices and has its own consequences, and we shall soon see what those consequences are.

If we ask which world these lovers resonate to, we need only return to the tall pine-tree and listen to Tristan:

> "This is not the enchanted orchard. But, one day, friend, we shall go together to a fortunate land from which none returns. There rises a castle of white marble; at each of its thousand windows burns a lighted candle; at each a minstrel plays and sings a melody without end. . . ."

This "enchanted orchard" is the inner world of psyche, the unexplored part of a human being outside of time and space. Of this world Tristan knows nothing until he drinks the love potion, but once he drinks it that world consumes him. His eyes are dazzled by what he has never before seen; his mind and body and all his senses are attuned ever after to only one level of existence.

But what about the King? What of Tristan's human life and duties? What of Iseult's marriage? her vows? her life with her husband? Here, under the pine-tree, we begin to sense that the love potion demands too much. It takes too much away. Unless we make it conscious, unless we put it on the correct level, it absolutely possesses us and dominates us from the depths; it dissolves our human lives, relationships, and commitments; it leaves nothing in their place. The world it opens tc us is rare and wonderful; it is a part of ourselves we long have needed to rediscover and touch. But as with every powerful new truth emerging from the unconscious, the love potion finds its way into places it does not belong, destroys things that should be saved, claims more than is its due.

When the love potion seizes Tristan and Iseult, it not only asks of them that they add a new dimension to their lives, it demands that they obliterate all sense of right and wrong, all the standards of loyalty, commitment, and faithfulness by which we ordinary mortals keep our lives and our human relationships intact upon the face of this earth.

We saw one drink of the love potion turn their world upside down. Now we see that it reverses morality: It reverses our values, turning right into wrong and wrong into right. Since the ascendancy of romantic love, most Westerners are torn constantly between two opposing ideals: One is the ideal of romance; the other is the ideal of commitment in human relationships. We commonly think they are the same, but they are utterly opposed.

With courtly love a whole new set of values came into our culture. Without our being aware, a new morality was born within us and began to shape our attitudes. Romance, in its purest form, seeks only one thing—passion. It is willing to sacrifice everything else—every duty, obligation, relationship, or commitment—in order to have passion. With courtly love we began to believe that the most important thing in life is to search for one's soul through romantic projection. We have not learned that there is any other way to find our soul. Our ideal of romance teaches us that we must seek the ultimate ecstasy, discover the "enchanted orchard," by the one means known to us: falling "in love."

The cult of romance legislates a new definition of "good" and "bad." Our new morality says that there is nothing so important as to be "in love," to feel that intensity and that ecstasy, to believe that one has once again found one's missing soul revealed in the beloved. Passion is the way—the only way—to wholeness and fulfillment. Passion is the one lane into the lost world of the gods.

Believing this, we could not help but enact a new standard of right and wrong: Whatever comes from being "in love" is "right"; whatever serves my passion is right; and whatever stands in the way of my passion must be shoved aside for the higher "good." We all answer with Tristan: "You that sit in judgment upon us here, do you know what cup it was we drank upon the high sea?" We believe that we have the right to follow our projections wherever they may lead and to pursue passion for its own sake, regardless of the relationships that are broken, regardless of the people who are hurt. Passion has become unconsciously defined as our highest good, our main goal in life; and all other values are commonly sacrificed to it.

Typically, a modern man will begin a marriage with his soul-image projected on his wife; he only begins to know his wife as a woman after the projection begins to lift. He finds that he loves her as a woman, he values her and respects her, he feels the beauty of being committed to her and knowing that she is committed to him. But one day he meets a woman who catches the projection of anima. He knows nothing of anima and less of projection; he only knows that this "other woman" seems like the essence of perfection; a golden light seems to envelop her, and his life feels exciting and meaningful when he is with her.

On that day, the two opposing armies in the Western psyche take up their swords and go to war within him. The two moralities begin their duel. On one side, his "human" morality tells him that it is wrong to betray his wife and set off on a course that will break his relationship. His instincts warn him to affirm what he has, to cherish the durable love that nourishes him, the stability and mutual trust that he and his wife have achieved.

But on the other side of his unconscious mind, another voice is heard: the morality of romance. Romance tells him that his life will only have meaning if he goes after anima, and that he must pursue his soul specifically in the body of the "other woman"—nothing less will do, for there lies passion, and passion is all. The morality of the love potion tells him he must seek passion at all costs: He has a "right" to fall "in love" at random; that is what life is all about! He has an affirmative "duty" to himself to get all the excitement and intensity that he can. The ancient voices of Cathars and courtly knights and ladies all whisper in unison that "true love" is found neither in marriage nor within ordinary relationship, that "true love" is only found with a woman other than his wife—a woman whom he sees not as *woman* but as the image of the goddess.

Such is the morality that envelops Tristan; such is the law by which he lives, whether trysting beneath the tall pine-tree or wandering the wild forest paths with Iseult. The only voice we hear raised in objection is the gruff voice of old Ogrin:

> "A man that is traitor to his lord is worthy to be torn by horses and burnt upon the faggot, and wherever his ashes fall no grass shall grow. . . . Lord Tristan, give back the Queen to the man who espoused her lawfully according to the laws of Rome. . . . Do penance, Tristan."

Here is a charming and quaint old man, a voice from ancient times. The old law sounds strange coming from his mouth. We are tempted to laugh and dismiss his exhortations as the hopelessly naive, old-fashioned morality of the bygone era.

But behind every ideal of morality is something worth looking at: a set of human values. Those values are not arbitrarily fabricated out of thin air, they come from somewhere in the depths of the human psyche and they answer to genuine human needs. Morality all too soon becomes a superficial social system, a calcified fossil that has lost touch with the real needs of people and that sets up arbitrary rules. But we can look behind the artificiality and discover the real needs that are served.

Underneath his quaint words, the old hermit pleads desperately for the qualities of loyalty and commitment—especially within marriage. Orgin cries out that human beings have to be able to depend on each other. He is saying that human life can't go on, relationships can't stay together, people can't really live out their love for one another in any meaningful way, unless human beings will truly honor the commitments they make to one another. Ogrin knows that Tristan and Iseult have not only thrown out sexual faithfulness, they have given up all loyalty, all commitment, all duty, save one—their dedication to passion.

But a commitment to passion is not a substitute for commitment to a human being. In our culture we have these two feelings completely confused. We are all committed to finding passion, we are all committed to being eternally "in love"; and we imagine that this is the same thing as being committed to a person. But the passion fades; the passion migrates to someone else we feel attracted to. If we are committed only to follow where passion leads, then there can be no true loyalty to an individual person.

Loyalty and commitment are archetypes in our human structure. They are as necessary to us as food and air. It is out of this profound human need for stable, loyal, and enduring relationships that the morality of Ogrin, the morality of commitment, grows.

Almost everyone is looking for "committed relationship." Most people sense that this is what they need, and people talk and read about "relationship" incessantly. But for all our talk about "commitment," we are sabotaged by our assumptions before we begin. We assume that the single ingredient that we need for "relationship," the one thing it cannot do without, is romance. But in fact, the essential ingredients for relationship are affection and commitment. If we look clearly, we begin to see that romance is a completely different energy system, a completely distinct set of values, from love and commitment. If it is romance that we seek, it is romance that we shall have—but not commitment and not relationship.

A man is committed to a woman only when he can inwardly affirm that he binds himself to her as an individual and that he will be with her even when he is no longer "in love," even when he and she are no longer afire with passion and he no longer sees in her his ideal of perfection or the reflection of his soul. When a man can say this inwardly, and mean it, then he has touched the essence of commitment. But he should know that he has an inner battle ahead of him. The love potion is strong: The new morality of romance is deeply ingrained in us; it seizes us and dominates us when we least expect it. To put the love potion on the correct level, to live it without betraying his human relationships, is the most difficult task of consciousness that any man can undertake in our modern Western world.

Here, then, are the two moralities that we find in conflict beneath the tall pine-tree: the morality of romance, and the morality of human commitment. Within each of us two armies from the ancient past are drawn up in ghostly array, fighting still the interminable battles of a past millennium. In this war there can be no resolution by battle, for emblazoned on the banner of each troop is a truth that we need, that must not be lost or destroyed.

But these two armies will clash and destroy until we finally learn on what level to live each truth. The truth hidden in the morality of romance is that of the soul, the inner world, the true "enchanted orchard"; it must be lived inwardly. The truth hidden in the morality of Ogrin is that of human loyalty and commitment; it is to be lived outwardly, on the level of our relationships with other people.

Our role is to be the peacemakers and the level-seekers—to find the level on which each truth is to be experienced and to live it affirmatively. When each need is honored and each world within us is honored, those ancient armies will put down their swords; they will make peace.

12

The Fourth Year of Morois

The spell of the love potion was to last for three years:

> La mere Yseut, qui le bollí,
> A trois Anz d'amistié le fist.

"The mother of Iseult who brewed it, for three years of love she made it"—so said the poet Béroul in the first and oldest tale of Tristan and Iseult.

It is no mere happenstance that the spell lasts for three years. It is no accident that Tristan and Iseult leave the Forest of Morois in the fourth year. Numbers are symbols: The numbers three and four represent particular stages of consciousness. Four is a symbol of wholeness, unity, and completion. The four elements, the four directions, the four seasons, the four divisions of the mandala—all were universal symbols of the unification of consciousness before historical time began. In dreams and myths, the occurrence of four—whether four objects, four people, or time divided into four—shows that a unification is possible, that the psyche is moving toward a synthesis or that an evolution is drawing toward completion. A new level of consciousness is possible, if one will pay the price; a new beginning is at hand.

By contrast, three is the symbol of incompleteness—that stage of consciousness in which we are aware that we are incomplete, that we don't know ourselves, but are unable as yet to solve the riddle of life. Three is dynamic, never at rest, always searching for the missing element, the unknown fourth member of the quaternity. Three is the stage in which we are not yet conscious of ourselves as a wholeness or a totality. We strive and we search, looking for the meaning, the answer, the unseen path to our true selves. Three becomes four by the addition of the missing part of our life, and four can become one: the consciousness of our wholeness and individuality as fact.

We see Blanchefleur languish three days after the death of Tristan's father, and on the fourth day Tristan is born. We hear the Morholt shout three times from the islet where Tristan is fighting him; then his fate is accomplished. We will yet see three and four repeated many times in our myth, even in the last moment of Tristan's life.

For three years Tristan and Iseult abide in the Forest of Morois. But in that wood they live as under a spell. We see them living like wild creatures—faces pallid and drawn, clothes torn and ragged from brambles—eating wild game and roots. Yet they are unaware of their hardships, for they are drunk with a magic wine, drunk with the sight of one another, awake only to their mutual dream. The lovers believe Morois to be the whole of life, to be the "enchanted orchard." But we who stand watching know that the projections of romance are not the whole of life, they only seem to be. The lovers dwell under the sign of three, and we know that outside the forest is a wider world.

When three years have passed, the spell is suddenly broken. The unseen clock of evolution pauses in its slow ticking and strikes the hour: It is the fourth year of Morois. King Mark miraculously walks into their tiny hut; he leaves his sword and his ring as tokens of his law and his love. He calls Tristan back to ordinary human life. He calls Iseult, Tristan's soul, back to her place in the inner world, back to reign beside him. An evolution has run its course; it is time to bring it to fruition, time for a new life to be revealed.

Every man, when he falls "in love," escapes into the Forest of Morois. He focuses his whole being on his fantasy of romance, for he believes that in his projection he has "found himself" and found all the wholeness of life. But, unknown to him, he is cut off from the world in the mists of Morois, lost for a time in the fogs of his projections. In Morois Wood he lives neither with the woman he married nor with anima whom he seeks: He lives for a time only with the *projection* of anima—an image radiant to his eye yet phantasmal, fading even as he holds her in his arms only to reappear half hidden among the trees, behind the rock, or in the mists above the waters. In this he has no choice, for he is possessed utterly by the love potion. But inevitably comes the moment, in the fullness of time, when the spell is broken.

Tristan awakes from a dream—a dream of three years. He discovers that even in his sleep the King has come to him. The King's tokens of reconciliation put Tristan in mind of the human world, a world he had forgotten—friendships, interests, work, duty, enthusiasms, people, relationships—all that is outside the "enchanted orchard." Tristan decides that he must return the Queen to the King, to her life, to her "palace hung with fine silks."

This is the exact point where a man has, for the first time, a chance to graduate out of his projections and into relationship. The spell is broken! The King comes to claim his own! A new era is dawning if he will see it and accept it. This is the evolution symbolized by the four; this is the awesome possibility that fate delivers to him. Freed of the potion, a man has the chance to see that the woman he loves and the projections he casts over her are separate realities. He has the opportunity to learn that his projections are really parts of himself: potentialities within him that he has never touched and never known because he has always tried to live them through a woman.

This fourth year of Morois yields a double revelation. The withdrawal of romantic projections also gives him the power to see woman as she is, to relate to her and value her as a person rather than as the carrier of his lost soul and of his unlived life. It opens the possibility of relating to a woman as an individual, as an equal, as a being in her own right. It enables him to begin to know her as she is, in all her complexity, in all her strengths and gifts—so different from his own and yet so necessary for his world.

Strangely, most men react to this stage of romantic love—this breaking of the spell—as though it were a great misfortune! It is the crucial point in an evolution, the opening of a wonderful possibility; but somehow he convinces himself that it is a disaster.

When a man's projections on a woman unexpectedly evaporate, he will often announce that he is "disenchanted" with her; he is disappointed that she is a human being rather than the embodiment of his fantasy. He acts as though she had done something wrong. If he would open his eyes, he would see that the breaking of the spell opens a golden opportunity to discover the real person who is there. It is equally the chance to discover the unknown parts of himself that he has been projecting on her and trying to live through her.

Faced with the new era, Tristan reacts as most men do; he bemoans his unhappy fate: "He will take away the Queen! How will I live?" He believes that if he can't have Iseult by projection, then he can't have her at all.

The crucial thing to be understood is this: Tristan is not losing a woman; nor is he losing anima. All of this commotion is over one issue: On what level is he going to live with anima? Is he going to retrieve his soul to himself? Is he going to live it as part of his own self? Will he take responsibility for his own unlived life? To return soul to the inner King means exactly that: to begin taking responsibility for living his own soul, rather than delegating that task to a woman.

This issue is always painful for the modern man. He is so accustomed to his pattern of trying to live out his unlived self through other people that the prospect of giving it up seems a disaster. He feels that all the joy and intensity of life is contained in the hope that one day a woman will come along who will make him whole and make life perfect. It is hard for him to see that he could live with a woman and be close to her and yet not try to live his life through her.

The issue is equally difficult for women. Many women are ready to rise up in rebellion over being put in the perpetual role of housekeeper, child-bearer, and servant. But few women object to being made the screen on which men project anima. Our culture trains women that their role is not to be human beings but to be mirrors who reflect back to a man his ideal or his fantasy. She must struggle to resemble the current Hollywood starlets; she must dress and groom herself and behave in such a way as to make herself into the collective image of anima. She must not be an individual so much as the incarnation of men's fantasy.

Many women are so accustomed to this role that they resist any change in the arrangement. They want to go on playing the goddess to a man rather than be a mortal woman: There is something appealing about being worshiped and adored as a divinity. But there is a heavy price attached to this role. The man who sees her as a goddess is not related to her as a woman; he is only related to his own projection, his own inner divinity that he has placed on her. And when his projection lifts, when it migrates away from her to some other woman, then his adoration and his worship will go with it. If he has no relationship to her as one human being to another, then there is nothing left when the projections evaporate.

Most people sense this, and so they spend tremendous energy and time finding ways to keep the projections going between them, ways to keep the fantasy quality alive between them and to hang onto the feeling of superhuman intensity. When people talk of techniques for "keeping the romance in marriage," "keeping the excitement in your relationship," or "making sure your spouse stays in love with you," they are assuming that the only possible basis for a "relationship" must be the projections. They assume that once the projections are allowed to evaporate, there will be no more basis for a relationship or marriage, so most techniques for saving marriages turn out to be techniques for manipulating projections and keeping them alive. It does not occur to modern Western people that a relationship could be made between two ordinary, mortal human beings, that they could love each other as ordinary, imperfect people and could simply allow the projections to evaporate. Yet this is what is required. Ultimately, the only enduring relationships will be between couples who consent to see each other as ordinary, imperfect people and who love each other without illusion and without inflated expectations.

Projections are a law unto themselves. We can manipulate them; we can artificially stimulate them and keep them alive for a certain time. But there always comes a point at which the symbolic "three years" have passed, the spell of the love potion is broken, the projections lift. At that point, we are all Tristans, standing in Morois with an issue to face and some choices to make.

If a man graduates correctly out of the Forest of Morois, it opens up a new world for him. He discovers that there are parts of himself, potentialities and forces, that he can't live out through a woman. He discovers that he can't make woman the carrier of all his unlived life and his unrealized self. He finds that there are things that he must do by himself and for himself: He must have an inner life; he must serve values that have meaning for him; he must have interests and enthusiasms that well out of his own soul, that are not merely spin-offs of his life with woman. This is the naked sword that Tristan places between himself and Iseult. It is the consciousness of his own individuality, of his own life, distinct from the life he leads with woman.

To do this does not hurt his relationship with woman: On the contrary, it makes relationship possible. As he relieves his woman of the burden of carrying his soul for him, it becomes possible for the first time to see her as a woman, to relate to her in her individuality, her specialness, and her humanity. He realizes that she also has to be an individual, must have her own life and her own reason for being. Neither can she project all of herself onto him nor live her life through him nor spend the rest of her life as a foil for his unlived self.

An awesome potential is at stake in this evolution. It is the potential for being fully individual while also relating genuinely to a fellow human being. It is by leaving the Forest of Morois, by returning Iseult to the King, by putting his own soul back inside himself, that a man wakes up to the fact of his individuality. In becoming aware that there is a part of himself that can't be lived through another person, for which he must take responsibility on his own, he awakens to the unexpected extensity and complexity of his individual self. In turn, as he awakens to his own uniqueness, he becomes capable of relating directly to a woman in her individuality. The test of true individuation is that it include the capacity to relate to another person and to respect him or her as an individual.

Unfortunately, it is exactly at this point in our evolution, where our possibilities are richest, that most people miss their opportunity. Refusing to graduate from Morois, they instead find some winding path that will lead them back into the forest meadows of their own projections.

When a man realizes that he has been trying to live his life through another person, he usually misses the true implications and jumps to the wrong conclusions. He begins talking about separating from his wife in order to "find himself." He thinks of all the things he hasn't done during their marriage. He wants to have a purpose in life, he wants to realize some goals, for he feels that life is slipping away from him. He wants to go back to school, start a new career, improve himself, go on a diet, go places he has failed to go and do the things he had failed to do.

If he ever looked at these ideals objectively, he could see that he can do most of these things perfectly well within his marriage or his relationship. He doesn't have to invent an either/or proposition: "either my individuation or my marriage." The reason he hasn't done these things is neither that he is married nor that his wife stands in his way. The true reason is that he hasn't had the self-discipline or imagination to do them for himself. He has expected his wife to live his unlived life for him; he has expected her to complete his life and make it whole without his having to help himself. Then on the day when he suddenly realizes that he is incomplete, that he is unfulfilled, that he is doing nothing about his own development, he blames her rather than himself. He says she is "standing in his way," "dragging him down," preventing him from "being himself."

This attitude only perpetuates the cycles of projection. It leads back into the fogs and bogs of Morois

Wood. A man who takes this approach usually breaks up his relationship, makes proclamations about how he is going to change his life on his own, and then goes looking for another woman who will solve all his problems and make his life complete—effortlessly. He settles back into his rut of trying to live his unconscious self through a woman; he has changed the woman, but the pattern is the same, and it leads to the same way of life. His "individuality" turns out to be an evasion, a circular path back into the woods. If this man had stayed in his relationship or his marriage and taken responsibility for developing his individuality there, then he could have faced the issue squarely.

Our desperate need is to realize that we need both qualities in life: We need individuality and we also need relationship to a particular person. We can't have one at the expense of the other; no man can be fully an individual unless he is fully related, and his capacity for genuine relatedness grows in proportion as he becomes a complete individual. These two aspects of life are yoked together by a deep and ancient bond, for they are really two sides of the same archetype, two faces of the same reality.

This, then, is the great evolution that becomes possible in the fourth year of Morois, in the breaking of the spell. It is this marvelous potential for making a synthesis between individuality and relationship—for evolving out of the illusory conflict between these two powerful energies within us and living them in the unity of one human life.

Tristan is called to sacrifice. He thinks he is asked to sacrifice both anima and woman; but he is not. He is called only to sacrifice a way of approaching anima and a way of approaching woman. He is called to give up his precious claim to the right to live his soul by projection. He is called to give up his demand that woman bear his unconscious for him. If he could make that sacrifice, and make it cleanly, he would discover that what he thinks he has lost will be returned to him: His soul will be returned to him as an inner experience, and he will find that there is another Iseult, a mortal woman, who has been waiting for him all along, outside the Forest of Morois, just beyond the mists of his projective world.

This is the law of sacrifice: If a man will truly give up that which he possesses on the wrong level, it will be returned to him on a right level. If he will give up trying to live Iseult the Fair on the wrong level, he will find her returned to him on a correct and workable level. In fact, his bounty will be doubled, for he will find that there are two Iseults, each to be experienced in her own way. One is Iseult the image of his soul; the other is Iseult the woman.

Unfortunately, Tristan fails his sacrifice. At the last moment his masculinity and his resolution are too weak. He makes a secret arrangement with Iseult that he will stay nearby and meet her secretly. He takes her ring of green jasper as token of her pledge to run to him any time he calls, to again betray the King. He reserves to himself the right to put her back into the world of projection, to put their relationship back on the same old level, to start anew the cycles of intrigue, secret meetings, broken vows, and betrayals.

If Tristan would keep his word, if he would make a clean sacrifice, he could elevate his relationship with Iseult to a new level. But he renounces the sacrifice, he makes a secret exception, and the evolution is aborted. The symbol of that incomplete sacrifice is the ring of green jasper, for by that ring they seal their agreement to undo the sacrifice. We shall soon see what terrible tricks that green jasper ring will play before our story is ended.

It is every man's fate to reach a point in his life at

which the spell is broken and he is called out of the Forest of Morois. It is a time of decision and of sacrifice. The King calls us forth to make a new way of life with Iseult the Fair and a new way of life with woman.

When dealing with archetypal material like that portrayed in this myth, it is good to remember that an ideal is being expressed that may not always be translated directly into practical life. Just as the Roman view on contraception, the traditional view of divorce, and monogamy are ideal statements from which culture may take its guidelines, so also is the mythological ideal presented in Tristan and Iseult a lofty view that may not always be possible in the give and take of human affairs. A note from the *I Ching* is encouraging at this point:

> In China, monogamy is formally the rule, and every man has but one official wife. This marriage, which is less the concern of the two participants than of their families, is contracted with strict observance of forms. But the husband retains the right also to indulge his more personal inclinations. . . . Of course it is a most difficult and delicate matter, requiring tact on the part of everyone concerned. But under favorable circumstances this represents the solution of a problem for which European culture has failed to find an answer. Needless to say, the ideal set for woman in China is achieved no oftener than is the European ideal. (*I Ching*, p. 209)

From this delicate observation from ancient China we take courage that an ideal is a lofty beacon, but one not always attained.

PART IV

THE NARRATIVE

How Tristan Found Iseult of the White Hands and How Love and Death at Last Were Mixed

---

Now we return to the story of Tristan. We find him where we left him, wandering in far lands. Quitting Iseult and the land of Cornwall, "Tristan fled his sorrow through seas and islands and many lands." Without Iseult life was empty, a living death, and he longed for the death that would release his sorrow. Yet he clung to her memory, nourished his sorrow as though it were life itself, and refused all other women. He wandered afar in wars and adventures, ever driven, ever homeless.

"I am weary, and my deeds profit me nothing; my lady is far off and I shall never see her again. Or why for two years has she made no sign, or why has she sent no messenger to find me as I wandered? But in Tintagel Mark honors her and she gives him joy. . . . I in my turn, shall I never forget her who forgets me? Will I never find someone to heal me of my unhappiness?"

Tristan did not know it, but heaven soon would send an answer to his question.

Tristan rode into Brittany, and there he saw a grievous sight, for the land was wasted, the towns deserted, and the farms burned. A hermit told him, "Good knight, our King Hoël is trapped at his castle of Carhaix, besieged by his vassal, Count Riol of Nantes. And that traitor Riol lays waste the land." Then Tristan rode to the walls of Carhaix and called out to the King, "I am Tristan, King of Lyonesse, and Mark of Cornwall is my uncle. Since your vassal does you wrong, I come to offer my arms."

Now the King would not take Tristan in, for there was little food left in Carhaix, their cause was hopeless, and bitter defeat was not far off. But the King's young son, Kaherdin, said: "My father, this is a goodly knight. Let him in, since he is so brave, that he may share our fortunes and misfortunes."

Kaherdin received Tristan with honor, and treated him as friend and brother, and he showed him all the castle and its devices and dungeons. So, holding each other's hands, they came into the women's room where Kaherdin's mother and sister sat together, weaving gold upon English cloth and singing a weaving song. And Tristan bowed to them. Then Kaherdin said: "See, friend Tristan, how my sister's hands run thread of gold upon this cloth. Of right, sister, are you called 'Iseult of the White Hands.' "

But Tristan, hearing her name, was startled. He smiled and looked at her most gently.

Now the traitor, Count Riol, was camped with a great army three miles from Carhaix. At night the fires of his camps could be seen, and he surrounded and starved the castle. But from that day, Tristan and Kaherdin rode out to sortie every day with a few faithful knights. By stealth and daring they ambushed the enemy and always brought back booty: wagonloads of food and arms. Hope rekindled in Carhaix, and King Hoël's men fought with more spirit. Rumor spread among Riol's troops of two invincible knights who fought always side by side, and the traitor was troubled.

Kaherdin rode to battle by Tristan's side, and they stood their ground together. Each watched over the other and rode quickly to his aid. They returned happy from combats, talking of chivalry, noble deeds, love, and adventure. So a deep love grew between them, and they were closer than brothers, and they kept faith and tenderness, as history tells. Always, as Kaherdin rode with Tristan, he praised his sister, Iseult, to him for her beauty, her goodness, and her simplicity.

One day Count Riol assaulted Carhaix in force, with a great army and siege machines. But Tristan and Kaherdin led their knights out in daring attack before the walls. Tristan rode straight at Count Riol and fought him sword to sword, man to man, until Riol, his helmet split by Tristan's sword, cried mercy. Riol surrendered and called off his army; he entered Carhaix to beg mercy of King Hoël and there swore allegiance to the King.

Now when all this had passed, Kaherdin said to his father, "Sire, keep you Tristan. Let Tristan marry my sister, and be a son to you and a brother for me." So the King took counsel and said to Tristan:

"Friend, you have won my love. Now take my daughter, Iseult of the White Hands, who comes of Kings and Queens, and of Dukes before them in blood. Take her, she is yours."

And Tristan answered: "I will take her, Sire."

For Tristan forgot his sorrows; Tristan was alive again. He loved Iseult of the White Hands, for her goodness and her beauty. He loved his brother, Kaherdin; he had high deeds to do, and a king to serve. And so he said, "I will take her, Sire."

Lord Tristan married Iseult of the White Hands, Princess of Brittany, at the gate of the minster, and Iseult was joyful. Kaherdin's heart overflowed, and all the people rejoiced.

But that night, as his valets undressed him, a green

jasper ring fell off Tristan's finger and clattered loudly on the stone floor. To Tristan's ears that sound was as the pealing of the bells of doom. Tristan awakened; he gazed at the ring. He remembered Iseult the Fair, away in Cornwall. All at once, sorrow returned.

"Ah! Now does my heart tell me I have done wrong. It was in the forest that you gave me this ring, where you suffered hardship for my sake. How wrong was I to ever accuse you of treason, Iseult the Fair, for now have I betrayed you! I have married another. And now what pity I feel for my wife, for her trust and her simple heart. See how these two Iseults have met me in an evil hour! and to each I have broken faith!"

In the bridal bed, Tristan lay quiet and cold as a stone and could not bring himself to touch his new wife. Finally she asked, "My lord, in what have I angered you, or in what done amiss, that I deserve not even a kiss of my husband?"

Then Tristan made a story. He said that once, on his deathbed from a dragon wound, he swore a holy oath to the Mother of God: If she healed him he would, should he marry, neither kiss his bride nor take his pleasure of her for one year. He said, "I must keep my vow, or risk the anger of God Almighty." Iseult agreed, but the next day, when the servants placed the wimple of a married woman on her head, she sighed sadly to herself and thought how little in fact she deserved to wear it. And Tristan grew ever more quiet and mourned for Iseult the Fair and stared at the green jasper ring on his hand.

As time passed, Iseult of the White Hands could not keep the secret from Kaherdin, her brother. He learned the truth: Tristan had never made her the true wife of his body. Now, Kaherdin was first amazed, and then wrathful. He rode to Tristan and said:

"Though you be my most beloved friend and brother,

I can not let this humiliation pass. Now you must either make my sister your wife in truth or know that I challenge you and by arms will I acquit my sister of this dishonor." Then Tristan told Kaherdin what he had told no other man save Ogrin the Hermit. He told him of the quest for Iseult the Fair, how they drank the love potion on the high seas, of the pain and longing that wracked his mind and body through days and nights, of the time in the Forest of Morois, of the lepers and the stake, the vows exchanged, the green jasper ring. "Now I know that without Iseult the Fair I can neither live nor die, and the life I lead is a living death."

As Kaherdin listened he could not hold onto his anger. Finally, in pity he said, "Friend Tristan, God save any man from the sorrows you have borne! I will consider all this for three days, and then tell you my judgment in the matter."

When three days had passed, Kaherdin said to Tristan:

"Friend, I have taken counsel in my heart. Yes, you have told me the truth, the life you live in this land is frenzy and madness, and no good can come of it for either you or my sister, Iseult of the White Hands. Hear what I propose. We will travel together to Tintagel; you will see the Queen and learn whether she still regrets you and is faithful to you. If she has forgotten you, then perhaps you will hold in greater fondness my sister Iseult, the gentle-hearted, the simple. I will follow you: am I not your peer and your comrade?"

"Brother," said Tristan, "well has it been spoken: 'The heart of a man is worth all the gold in a country.' "

Kaherdin and Tristan disguised themselves as pilgrims and sailed across to Cornwall. Tristan sent the green jasper ring to Iseult with a message that she meet him. But Iseult the Fair was in a quandary: She had heard the news of Tristan's marriage to Iseult of the White Hands. She believed that Tristan had betrayed her, preferred another woman to her. Yet she had promised! . . . What should she do? She arranged to meet Tristan; but then she heard more rumors of betrayal. Finally, when Tristan came to her, disguised as a beggar, she told her valets to beat him and drive him away. So Tristan left in sorrow and sailed with Kaherdin to Brittany. But Iseult, hearing that Tristan left in despair, knew that she must have been wrong. Weeping bitterly, she spent the long nights and days in penance and remorse.

In Carhaix Tristan languished; neither his wife nor adventures nor the hunt nor life itself held any charm for him. Finally he said, "I must return to see her, for rather would I die seeing her one more time than die here of longing for her. Who lives in sorrow is like a man dead already, and I would that I might die, but that the Queen might know that it was for love of her that I die. If only I might know that she suffered for me even as I suffer for her!"

Tristan dressed again as a pilgrim and, without telling Kaherdin, made his way back to Tintagel. He rubbed his face with mud and pretended to be a clown, a fool, a crazed traveling jester. Coming before King Mark's Court, he called out to the King: "Give to me the Queen Iseult, and I will hold her and serve you for her love."

Laughing, the King asked, "And where would you take her, O Fool?"

"Oh! very high, between the clouds and heaven, into a fair chamber glazed. The beams of the sun shine through it, yet the winds do not trouble it at all. There would I bear the Queen into that crystal chamber of mine, all compact of roses and the morning."

Playing the madman, Tristan later made his way into the Queen's chambers and showed her the green jasper ring. At first suspicious, she finally recognized him and fell into his arms. Crazed with desire, he returned again and again for three days to have his fill with her, until the guards grew so suspicious that he knew he must leave or be caught.

"Friend, I must fly, for they are wondering. I must fly, and perhaps shall never see you more. My death is near, and far from you my death will come of desire."

"O friend," she said, "fold your arms round me close and strain me so that our hearts may break and our souls go free at last. Take me to that happy place of which you told me long ago. The fields whence none return, but where great singers sing their songs forever. Take me now."

"I will take you to the Happy Palace of the Living, Queen! The time is near. When it is finished, if I call you, will you come, my friend?"

"Friend," said she, "call me and you know that I shall come."

With that prophecy of death Tristan rushed away, and Iseult never saw him again as living man.

Tristan returned to Carhaix, but still he refused to touch his wife, and never did human happiness light his eyes or joy show in his face. After a time he rode to the aid of Kaherdin, who did battle with an enemy baron. They were ambushed, and though Kaherdin and Tristan slew all seven knights who beset them, Tristan was pierced with a poisoned spear. For the last time in his life, Tristan fell with deadly poison in his veins, and neither doctor nor magician could find the cure. But Tristan called Kaherdin to him and said:

"Brother, for me there is no cure. Take you this green jasper ring and go to Iseult the Fair. Show it her, and tell her if she does not come I die; say she *must* come *for we drank our death together and to remember the oath I swore to serve a single love, for I have kept that oath."*

Now this was the signal they agreed on: If Kaherdin returned with Iseult the Fair he should show a white sail, but if she refused to come, then a black sail.

"Fair comrade, do not weep," said Kaherdin, "for I will do what you desire."

But Iseult of the White Hands listened at the door and almost fainted at what she heard. For the first time she understood why her husband had so rejected her. From that day on, though she made no sign, she only meditated bitterly on her revenge—revenge against Iseult the Fair, who had robbed her of both husband and earthly happiness.

Kaherdin took a ship and sailed straight to Tintagel with fair winds following. He came to the King's court as a merchant and, showing the queen his wares, put before her a green jasper ring. Then he whispered Tristan's message. Straightaway the Queen quit the castle and secretly boarded Kaherdin's ship; the ship sailed at the tide, and Iseult watched the bow cut through foamy waves, and her gaze was ever toward Carhaix.

Tristan was so weak he could no longer watch on the sea cliffs by Carhaix. But each day, as he lay on his pallet, he asked of his wife if she saw the ship returning. Until one day she looked to sea and saw the ship, its white sail billowing before the wind. Then, in the bitterness of her heart, she took her revenge. Coming to her husband, she said:

"My lord, the ship is in sight."

"And the sail," asked Tristan, "what is the manner of the sail?"

"Why, for its color," she said, "it is black."

Tristan turned to the wall.

"I can not keep this life of mine any longer," he said.

Then he said slowly, "Iseult, my friend." He repeated it slowly four times, and on the fourth time he died.

But at sea the wind rose; it struck the sail fair and drove the ship to shore, and Iseult the Fair set foot upon the land. She heard loud mourning in the streets and the tolling of bells in the minsters and the chapel towers; she asked the people the meaning of the knell and of their tears. An old man said to her:

"Lady, we suffer a great grief. Tristan, that was so loyal and so right, is dead. It is the chief evil that has ever fallen on this land."

She went up to the palace, following the way, and her cloak was random and wild. The Bretons marveled as she went; nor had they ever seen woman of such a beauty, and they said:

"Who is she, or whence does she come?"

Near Tristan, Iseult of the White Hands crouched, maddened at the evil she had done, and calling and lamenting over the dead man. The other Iseult came in and said to her:

"Lady, rise and let me come by him; I have more reason to mourn him than you—believe me."

And when she had turned to the east and prayed God, she moved the body a little and lay down by Tristan, beside her friend. She kissed his mouth and his face, and clasped him closely; and so gave up her soul, and died beside him of grief for her lover.

When word came to King Mark, he crossed the sea and brought them home to Cornwall and made them each a fine tomb, to the left and right of a chantry. One night a briar bush sprang from Tristan's tomb. Strong were its branches, green its leaves, and fragrant its flowers. Quickly it climbed over the chantry and descended to root close by Iseult's tomb. And for many lives of men it endured, strong and lovely and fragrant.

13

Puzzles and Paradoxes

We have gone the whole journey with Tristan and Iseult. We have stood close by and seen them through joys, sufferings, and finally, death. But our journey is not yet over, for we must make this journey twice: once to experience it, once to learn and understand. Now our task is to step back and ask: What does this mean? What lesson is here for me?

In this last, most dramatic portion of the story, there are some puzzles, some questions, some paradoxes. We need to look at them now and get them clear in our minds. Then, as we move ahead through the symbols, we can bear them in mind and refer back to them.

The first and most glaring paradox is Tristan's rejection of Iseult of the White Hands. As this part of our story begins, we find Tristan wandering in deep despair and loneliness. He cries out: "Will I never find someone to heal me of my unhappiness?"

Soon his question is answered. He finds Iseult of the White Hands, Kaherdin, a king to serve, a decent human life to live. But then he refuses it! Why? It makes no human sense. He failed to make a human relationship to Iseult the Fair; he has returned her to King Mark, and Iseult the Fair has her own life there. Why, then, will he not make a human life with Iseult of the White Hands?

By what strange morality, what strange notions of "right" and "wrong," "faithfulness" and "betrayal," does he believe that he must condemn himself to perpetual suffering and aloneness? Why does he believe it is his duty to reject the woman he lives with and die of longing for an idealized goddess whom he carries in his mind but whom he can never truly possess in this physical life?

Humanly this makes no sense, for such an attitude destroys human life: It literally reduces Tristan's life to a "living death." Yet, to the romantic part of us, Tristan's attitudes make perfect sense. A voice within each man insists fervently that it is a wonderful thing to search forever for the perfect idealized feminine, rather than settle for the flesh-and-blood woman that real life has put into his arms.

Every psychologist has a steady stream of patients who repeat Tristan's question: "Will I never find someone to heal me of my unhappiness?" It is the most often asked question in our society. Yet most men follow Tristan's pattern. When a flesh-and-blood, mortal human appears in a man's life who offers him love and relatedness, he ends in rejecting her because she can't measure up to the idealized perfection—Iseult the Fair—who can only live in his inner mind.

The second grand puzzle in this part of our story is this: What is this "love" that exists between Tristan and Iseult the Fair? As we follow along with them we are very credulous most of the way; after all, we are Western romantics. But finally we begin to wonder at the blatant egocentricity, the whims that they visit upon each other in the name of "love"!

Tristan complains of Iseult that "Mark honors her and she gives him joy!" Why, if Tristan loves her so, does he not want her to be happy with her husband? This may seem a naive question, but if Tristan pretends to be motivated by "love," we have the right to ask it. Later he says, "I would that I might die, but that the Queen might know that it was for love of her that I die. If only I might know that she suffers for me as I suffer for her!"

What kind of "love" is this, whereby Tristan wants his beloved, not to be happy, but to suffer? If he believes that she has made peace with the past and is happy with King Mark, why does Tristan return to throw fuel on the flames of her passion? Why does he seek to renew her suffering, to upset her life with King Mark?

And what of Iseult? What is this "love" that moves her to despise Tristan because he has married another woman? Iseult is married to King Mark and lives with him. Yet by these strange standards, Tristan may not marry another woman, may not love another woman; above all, he may not be happy. If he does any of these normal human things, then it is a "betrayal" of Iseult the Fair! What kind of "love" makes Iseult want Tristan to be alone and miserable, to have no wife, no home, no children?

This is not love. Love is a feeling that is directed to another human being, not at one's own passion. Love desires the well-being and happiness of one's beloved, not a grand drama at the expense of the other person. Yet, strangely, Tristan and Iseult call this "love."

By human standards, it is all backwards: They "love" each other, yet each wants the other to suffer, to be unhappy. They speak of "betrayal," but their way of being "faithful" to each other is to betray Iseult's husband and Tristan's wife. They have refused to set up a household and make a human life together, yet neither will allow the other to live in a normal human fashion with someone else.

All this is not really new to us. We have all seen

people act this way who were "in love." Most of us have lived out these same contradictory attitudes. We sometimes manage to be slightly more subtle about it, but the paradox shows forth blatantly in the myth because it comes raw and fresh from the unconscious.

As we work through our symbols it will become increasingly clear that the greatest paradox is romantic love itself: As a system of attitudes, it is the parent from which these curious contradictions emanate. Romantic love is an unholy muddle of two holy loves. One is "divine" love, of which we have spoken before: It is our natural urge toward the inner world, the soul's love of God, or the gods. The other is "human" love, which is our love for people—flesh-and-blood human beings. Both of these loves are valid; both are necessary. But by some trick of psychological evolution our culture has muddled the two loves in the potion of romantic love and nearly lost them both.

At its best romanticism and romantic love are valid attempts to restore to Western consciousness what has been lost. Romanticism seeks to restore our sense of the divine side of life, the inner life, the power of imagination, myth, dream, and vision. The tragedy that this portion of our story shows us is that we misuse the ideal of romanticism, misplace the divine love, and in the process we destroy our human relationships. We call "love" what is not love, we reverse the meaning of "faithfulness," and we pursue an ephemeral idealized image of anima, rather than loving a flesh-and-blood human being.

But here is a caveat: As we look at some of the awful implications of the tragedy that *Tristan and Iseult* becomes, we need to remember that romantic love is a necessary stage in our psychological evolution. Whatever may be said against it, whatever we have to do to straighten out our relationship to it, it is our path: our

Western way to evolving and refining the two loves that we have mixed in the love potion. Romantic love is like a "tunnel of love": We can't get stuck there in the dark; we have to come out the other side and resolve the paradox. But for Westerners it seems necessary to enter the tunnel. The only way we know to find feeling, to approach the two great loves, is to "fall in love," to be crucified in the paradox and learn.

As we move ahead, as we unmask illusions and expose contradictions, let us remember that the question is not whether we should praise romantic love or condemn it, keep it or throw it away. Our task is to make it a path to consciousness, to live the paradox honestly, to learn how to honor both of the worlds contained in romantic love: the divine world of Iseult the Fair that Tristan pursues, and the human world of Iseult of the White Hands that he rejects.

14

Iseult of the Earth

Tristan never makes a human relationship to Iseult the Fair. He never makes a committed, stable, day-to-day life that would give them the human warmth and companionship that each needs. It startles us to realize this when we think of all the dramas and adventures they pass through. They meet in secret, they take terrible risks, they are dragged to the stake, they escape, they continue the drama in the Forest of Morois—struggling with nature and with enemies. Yet all this never translates into a human relationship!

One of the great paradoxes in romantic love is that *it never produces human relationship as long as it stays romantic.* It produces drama, daring adventures, wondrous, intense love scenes, jealousies, and betrayals; but people never seem to settle into relationship with each other as flesh-and-blood human beings until they are out of the romantic love stage, until they *love* each other instead of being "in love."

We begin to understand why this is so. Iseult the Fair is anima. It is the divine love that Tristan seeks in her; unconsciously he seeks passage to the inner world. Tristan can not make an ordinary human relationship to Iseult the Fair because she is anima and must be experienced as inner person, as symbol.

When Tristan departs Cornwall, leaving Iseult with King Mark, he falls into despair. He believes that he leaves anima, literally embodied in a mortal woman, just as all men do when they are "in love." In his ego's view, life has no meaning, for he thinks that meaning can only be found in Iseult the Fair.

> Apart the lovers could neither live nor die, for it was life and death together; and Tristan fled his sorrow through seas and islands and many lands.

And so comes Tristan's famous question: "Will I never find someone to heal me of my unhappiness?"

Although his ego sees it as death, fate draws him onward toward life itself! For the quiet, unassuming woman who awaits him in Carhaix Castle is the incarnation of human life: She is Iseult of the White Hands, Iseult of the Earth.

Like Tristan, we come to this Iseult burdened with prejudices, with prior claims on our loyalty. We don't like anything that is "simple": To us "simple" means dull or dense or stupid. We have forgotten that simplicity is a need in human life: It is the human art of finding meaning and joy in the small, natural, and less dramatic things. At its highest, it is a consciousness that sees through the confusions we invent to the essential, uncomplicated reality of life. But in our era, we have a collective prejudice against Iseult of the White Hands. If a direct, uncomplicated, simple relationship offers us happiness, we won't accept it. It is "too simple," "too dull." We are trained to respect only what is inflated, hyperintense, high-pressured, big and complicated.

The true tragedy of *Tristan and Iseult* is hidden in a quiet, humble place where we are not likely to look. It is not Tristan's death, for all men die. Tristan's tragedy is that he refuses to live while he is yet alive, and so he has no human life or human love. This is how his life becomes a "living death." The real tragedy occurs in that moment when Tristan refuses Iseult of the White Hands; in that act he refuses the earth and all that comes with this earthly human life—human love, relatedness, all of earth's joys.

For us Westerners, who imbibe the liquor of romance with our mothers' milk, Iseult of the White Hands seems a minor player. We are mesmerized by the other drama: the secret meetings and partings, the intrigues, the unearthly intensity that rages between Tristan and Iseult the Fair. But if we step back from that and turn our gaze on Iseult of the White Hands, it may be as Kaherdin said: "Then perhaps you will hold in greater fondness my sister, Iseult the gentle-hearted, the simple."

This Iseult personifies a different side of the inner feminine, a side we have not met before. Her "white hands" connote many things in symbol. They are fair and delicate, yet skilled in the practical work of life. This Iseult delights in the ordinary, human, earthly life. We find her first in the women's room of the castle; she is weaving tapestries, working gold into fine English cloth. She is of royal blood, yet we can imagine her bearing children, rearing them, cooking, living with the simple activities that make human life possible.

We will call this aspect of the feminine the "earth feminine," for it is she who relates a man to this physical earth, to his fellow human beings, to ordinary life, to all that is part of being *incarnate* in this human realm bounded by necessity, commitment, duty, time, and space. The earth feminine is the inner person who empowers him to love on a human level, to make human relationships.

She personifies the capacity within each man for seeing the beauty, the value, and the sacredness in the physical world, in the physical life, and in ordinary humanness. It is she who presides over his relationships with *outer* persons in the *external* world. By contrast, anima presides over his relationship to the *inner* persons of the *interior* realm. The earth feminine knows how to love in a way that is neither romantic idealism nor a projection of inner gods out onto external mortals. Hers is a human love that relates us to flesh-and-blood women and men, that affirms them in their humanness and ordinariness.

Everything that Iseult of the White Hands does show us that her one concern is relatedness. That is her one principle, her fundamental energy system. Tristan says of Iseult the Fair: "We drank our Death together." But this Iseult is not interested in death: She is interested in life, an ordinary human life on this earth with a person who will love her as she is, care for her, and be nurtured by her. This Iseult of the Earth does not ask to be taken to the "enchanted orchard" found only in the land of death; rather, she asks Tristan to love her and make a life with her in the here-and-now of Carhaix, during their lives on this earth.

We see the earth feminine more clearly as we contrast Iseult of the White Hands with Iseult the Fair. We can not imagine Iseult the Fair as housewife, rearing children, stirring pots of soup, weaving blankets, growing old with her husband in a simple household. We can only imagine her as part of a great drama, dangerous encounters, ecstatic meetings, tearful partings, or as Queen, enthroned in a fairy castle. She is a sorceress, daughter of a sorceress queen, born on a mystic isle across the Unknown. She is goddess: half divine, half person. She is that aspect of the feminine that must always be elusive, unattainable, the "faraway Princess" who can only be truly experienced on the level of the symbolic and imaginal. Anima can be lived inwardly, or she can be extroverted into a drama—

the stake, the lepers, the Wood of Morois. But she can't be contained in ordinary, simple human relationship with its duties, its finite limits.

But what of Iseult of the White Hands? She is human. She is not born of sorcerers and demigods in an outpost of the "other world." She is born in the known world of mortal parents, reared in ordinary human surroundings, prepared for a human life, a personal life. She is the aspect of the feminine that fits into our ordinary lives and personal relationships.

Anima's desire is always to take us to the inner world, to the boundless and infinite reaches of the unconscious, with no limitations, no commitments to anyone, no holding back for the limits of necessity or duty. But the earth feminine directs us to the finite, the personal world of human relationship—that which is bounded by commitment, duty, obligation, affection, and relatedness to an individual.

As life turns to death, and death draws near, there is only one time when Tristan begins to live again. He draws near to Iseult of the White hands: he wants to live, he wants to love, and he wants to be human again. He forgets his strange pact with death. Kaherdin opens the gates of Carhaix and takes Tristan to his heart. Tristan finds affection, friendship, love, noble deeds to do.

"Will I never find someone to heal me of my unhappiness?" Here is a wife who loves him, who will give him companionship, devotion, a feeling life, erotic love, the human ties of home and family. With her comes a brother, a father, a homeland. Why does he reject all this?

Later in the story he tells us why. . . . Lying on his deathbed, he confides the green jasper ring to Kaherdin and sends him off on one last race to fetch Iseult the Fair.

"Say she must come, for we drank our death together, and to remember the oath I swore *to serve a single love,* for I have kept that oath."

It is this mistaken ideal, this oath, that underlies the whole tragedy of romantic love. Tristan swore to serve a *single love.* That single love is the divine love of which we have spoken: the love that draws us to the inner world. But when Tristan vows to serve only that divine love of anima, he vows also to give up human love and human relationship. There are two great loves, two worlds in which man must live, two Iseults whom he must serve. The great flaw in romantic love is that it seeks one love but forgets the other. This is the exact meaning of Tristan's rejection of Iseult of the White Hands.

When Tristan refuses Iseult of the White Hands he shows us the standard attitude of Western men. A Western man unconsciously believes that it is right for him to use his marriage to try to connect with his anima, to use a woman to carry his projected soul-image, and that he need not ever take a woman seriously in her own right, as a physical, individual being with her own complex structure and consciousness. A man believes that he must always search for Iseult the Fair and always reject Iseult of the White Hands; he must always seek the divine world that he projects on a woman but never relate to that woman as an individual person.

Romantic love, true to its paradoxical nature, fools us: It *looks as though* it aims at making a human relationship to a person. After all, one is not meditating in a temple; one is "in love" with a human person. Or is one? It is difficult for us to see the difference—the vast difference—between *relating* to a human person and *using* that person as a vehicle for one's projection.

In Tristan's vow, and in his refusal of his marriage, we find the basic flaw in romanticism: its partialness. It attempts to balance the one-sidedness of our Western psyche by restoring the experience of the gods, the inner world, the mysteries, and the divine love. But, like all collective attempts at balancing, it has become one-sided in the opposite direction. It embraces the opposite polarity, it idealizes the divine and ecstatic world but leaves no room for ordinary humanness. Ordinary human life, with its obligations, its ties, its commitments, it duties, its limitations, and its focus on ordinary human beings, is too earthbound, too dull and sordid for our romantic prejudices.

Tristan's marriage symbolizes his instinctive, involuntary embrace of human life and human relatedness. His instincts cry out for a down-to-earth, physical, loving companionship with an ordinary, mortal woman. King Hoël offers his daughter. Tristan answers, out of pure reflex and will-to-live, "I will take her, Sire." She is not his soul, she is not perfection, she is not a visitor from heaven. But she is beautiful in her human way, she is loving, she is related to him, and she is real. She is not his fantasy laid across the face of the external world.

But Tristan, having married Iseult in form, refuses her in fact. When he refuses to consummate the marriage, it means that he rejects human relationship with a mortal being in favor of a passionate vision, a fantasy that can only be experienced inwardly. This is the effect that the romantic ethos has on most modern marriages and relationships. We marry in form, we say the words, but we don't inwardly make the commitment. There is a provisional quality in most relationships; each person secretly writes an escape clause into it. Each of us reserves the right to break his or her commitment to this physical person if a passionate vision should happen to be projected on another person.

This is exactly what the myth was predicting for our

culture, and this is exactly what we see as the normal pattern. People make the marriage in form but refuse it in fact. They refuse to make a real commitment to a human being, because they will only commit themselves to their inner vision, their inner ideal, their search for the perfect manifestation of anima or animus, their search for the divine love. Since they have not learned that this is an *inner* task, they imagine that they must always keep their options open, they must always reserve the right to follow wherever the inner ideal is projected. In our romantic fog, we think this is very noble, very "liberated," but in fact it is just a misunderstanding of reality. It is our way of obliterating the human side of the equation, our way of refusing to be committed to Iseult of the White Hands.

The tragedy is that Tristan, in full possession of a life of relatedness, surrounded with human warmth, refuses to enjoy it or appropriate it. Curiously, there is nothing he need do: He only needs to open his eyes, wake up to the riches that surround him, and live. But that fog of romantic idealism, that denigration of the human world, cuts him off from the very love for which he starves. He rejects Iseult of the White Hands: He renews his pact with death.

This pattern in romantic love replays itself constantly in the lives of modern people. A man in a relationship or marriage feels vaguely dissatisfied: Life doesn't have enough meaning, or he misses the ecstasy and the "rush" that he used to feel. Instead of realizing that he is longing for the divine love, for the inner experience of anima that is his own responsibility, he finds fault with the woman. She is not making him happy; she is not good enough; she does not fulfill his dreams. Although she gives him everything that a mortal woman could provide, he rejects her and goes looking for Iseult the Fair. He always assumes that somewhere, in some woman or in some adventure, he is going to find Iseult the Fair and be able to possess her physically and find there his meaning and fulfillment. Thus we denigrate human love; thus we reject Iseult of the White Hands; thus we renew our collective vow to "serve a single love."

Human love, symbolized by Iseult of the White Hands, is utterly different from what we call "falling in love." For a man to love in the human way of the earth feminine means for him to direct his love to a mortal human being, not at the idealized image that he projects. It means for him to be related to the actual human being, to value her, to identify with her, to affirm her value and her sacredness *as she is,* in her totality—with her shadow side, her imperfections, and all that makes her an ordinary mortal. To be "in love" is different: It is not directed at a woman; it is directed at anima, at a man's ideal: his dream, his fantasy, his hope, his expectation, his passion for an inner being whom he superimposes over the external woman.

This explains why so much of this "love" between Tristan and Iseult the Fair is so unmistakably egocentric. Tristan wants Iseult to suffer, to join him in his unhappiness, because his love is not really directed at Iseult as a mortal woman, but at himself! He is concerned with *his* projection onto her, with *his* passion—this passion that he blames on the love potion but that he studiously nurtures with return trips to Iseult.

Iseult, similarly, seems not to be concerned with Tristan's happiness or well-being. She is concerned with whether he is putting her first, whether his allegiance is only to her, whether he will keep up the drama with her that transports her to the "enchanted orchard." Neither of them is concerned with the happiness or well-being or survival of the other but only with renewing their own passion, with being transported to a magical place, with using each other to keep the intense drama going. Finally, at the end, their only concern is to use each other to break free completely from the ordinary earth, to fly to that magical, imaginal world where "great singers sing their songs forever." They do not actually love each other. They use each other as vehicles to have the intense, passionate experiences they long for.

This, whether we admit it or not, is what romantic love is. In Tristan and Iseult the egotism, the use of each other to create the passion for its own sake, is so blatant, so naive, and so childlike that it is unmistakable. But our own versions of this are scarcely more subtle. It simply never enters our romantic heads that there is something strange about seeking a so-called "love" for the sake of *my* fulfillment, *my* thrills, *my* dreams coming true, *my* fantasy, *my* "need to be loved," *my* ideal of the perfect love, *my* security, *my* entertainment.

When we genuinely love another person, it is a spontaneous act of being, an identification with the other person that causes us to affirm, value, and honor him or her, to desire that person's happiness and well-being. In those rare moments when we are *loving,* rather than focused on our own egos, we stop asking what dreams this person is going to fulfill for us, what intense and extraordinary adventures he or she is going to provide.

There are two marriages that Tristan needs to make. The first marriage is an inner marriage with his own soul, with Iseult the Fair. That marriage is made by going to the inner world, practicing his religion, his inner work, living with the gods of the inner world. The second marriage is to Iseult of the White Hands. This marriage means a union with another human being, and it means taking her *as* a human being. It also means making other relationships—making friends—and taking them as human beings.

We can understand these two marriages as reflecting the two natures that combine in human beings: the human and the divine. The penultimate Western symbol of our two natures in synthesis is Christ, and the dimensions of that reality are expressed perfectly in the symbolism of the Christian doctrine of Incarnation. There, it is said that God came into the physical world and redeemed it; God becomes human! The implications of this belief, taken as symbol, are enormous. It means that this physical world, this physical body, and this mundane life we lead on this earth are also holy. It means that our fellow human beings have their own intrinsic value: They are not here merely to reflect our fantasy of a more perfect world or to carry our projections of anima or to join us in acting out an allegory of another world. The physical, mundane, ordinary world has its own beauty, its own validity, and its own laws to be observed.

There is a statement in Zen: "This earth—that is the Way!" The Way to enlightenment, to soul, is not through the clouds, not by denying this earth. It is found within this mortal life, within the simplicity of our mundane tasks and our relationships with ordinary people. All of this is expressed in the symbolic reality of the Incarnation.

The Incarnation tells us of the paradox of two natures: of divine love and human love mixed in one vessel, contained in one human being. The Incarnation says that God became Man; and the Incarnate God, Christ, was both fully human and fully divine. In this image is reflected the dual nature of every human, the two loves that legitimately claim our loyalty, and the synthesis we should make between the two. The Incarnation shows us that the divine world and the personal world coexist within each human being. It is when the two natures live together in a conscious synthesis that a person becomes a conscious self.

Whatever may be our ideas about the literal historical

Incarnation, we need to see the awesome implications of God-become-man as a symbol, as an archetypal model deep in the Western unconscious. It is a psychological reality, a unifying principle that acts on us from within, whether we be conscious of it or not. We are going to live this dual nature in one way or another, either consciously or unconsciously.

The Incarnation symbolizes the synthesis; the love potion symbolizes the muddle. If we take our dual nature consciously we get the transcendent synthesis; if we take it haphazardly, we get the love potion. Western psychological history is this: As we cease to take seriously the Incarnation, even as symbolic reality, the truth of our dual nature goes underground. Unconsciously, the divine love, and the whole paradox of divine love and human love, finds its way into the love potion. And there it rests today, bubbling in a cauldron of projection, mixed up in the soup of romantic love.

We learned that one of the cultural roots of romantic love is Manichaean dualism, living in western Europe in the twelfth century as the Albigensian heresy. The teaching of that religion was that the divine half of reality is absolutely good and the human side of reality is absolutely evil. For the Albigensians, the only good was what existed on the "spiritual" plane, what was found in "heaven." Physical human beings, ordinary human life, sexuality, erotic love, and this whole physical earth were seen as "evil," as a corrupt, steaming pit of darkness. This is the theological expression of what Tristan says in the language of romance: "Remember the oath I swore to serve a single love." Albigensian dualism, Christian dualism, and romantic idealism all teach us that we should only serve the divine love, that ordinary human beings are not worthy of our love, that we should love people only insofar as they reflect our ideal, reflect our projection of otherworldly intensity—the superhuman, cosmic, and divine.

The cult of romance teaches us that ordinary people are not enough, that we must seek a god or goddess, a Hollywood star, a dream-woman or dream-man, a beauty queen: an embodied anima or animus. So long as a man is caught in this mentality he will never accept anything except his anima; he relates to a woman only if she reflects his dream of Iseult the Fair.

The tale of Iseult of the White Hands is the tale of Tristan's lost opportunity. Tristan misses his chance to discover that there are two loves and two relationships: one with anima within and one with woman in the physical world. Each is distinct, and each has its own validity. But, if Tristan, like us, had a second chance, he could *learn* from Iseult of the White Hands rather than reject her. He could learn that the meaning of life is not found only in seeking his inner ideal; it is also found in the physical woman with whom he lives in the castle of Carhaix.

15

Suffering and Death

De tous les maux, le
mien diffère;
Il me plait; je me réjouis
de lui;
Mon mal est ce que
je veux
Et ma douleur est
ma santé!
Je ne vois donc pas de
quoi je me plains,
Car mon mal me vient
de ma volonté;
C'est mon vouloir que
devient mon mal,
Mais j'ai tant d'aise à
vouloir ainsi
Que je souffre
agréablement,
Et tant de joie dans
ma douleur
Que je suis malade avec
délices.

From all ills mine differs;
It pleasures me;
I rejoice in it;
My illness is what
I want
And my pain is my health!
I don't see, then,
of what I complain,
For my illness comes to
me of my own will;
It is my own wish
that becomes my ill,
But I find so much
pleasure in wishing thus
That I suffer
agreeably,
And so much
joy within my pain
That I am sick
with delight

—Chrétien de Troyes

These are the words of one of the greatest poets of the age of troubadours, the voice of one who first recorded some of the greatest "romances" in out early romantic literature. How perfectly he captures the strange, unacknowledged connection between romance and suffering! Suffering seems to be an inseparable part of romance, as every man and woman knows who has been in love. We can try to evade it, we sometimes imagine that we have escaped it, but it always awaits us in the place we least suspect. Even our word *passion* originally meant "to suffer."

The suffering is as though designed into romance by our ancestors, who, unlike us, actually saw romance as a spiritual discipline. By teaching us to seek, in a woman or a man, an ideal of perfection that could never be incarnated in mortal flesh, they sentenced us to a seemingly endless cycle of impossible expectations followed by bitter disappointments.

But there is more to it than that: It is also true that unconsciously we *seek* our suffering! Like Tristan, we seem unconsciously to go out of our way to set up impossible situations, to become involved with impossible people, to impose expectations on our relationships that can't possibly be met. We pursue our suffering as though it were a necessary part of romantic experience, as though we could not do without it. Unconsciously we seem to delight in it: "It pleasures me; I rejoice in it." If my wishes are impossible, if they bring me more pain than ecstasy, nevertheless, "I find so much pleasure in wishing thus that I suffer agreeably, and so much joy within my pain that I am sick with delight."

There is much to be learned by looking at the poetry and the romances of our ancestors, for they had the grace to state bluntly the truths that we are unwilling to face. If we can open our minds and learn from them to say what is, then we can begin to understand what forces are at work in us. It is no coincidence that all romantic literature, from *Tristan and Iseult* to *Romeo and Juliet* and up to the present, is filled with suffering and death. The very nature of romance seems to require that it be lived in the face of impossible odds, terrible obstacles, and inhuman adversities. Finding their romance impossible in this physical world, many of the archetypal lovers, like Romeo and Juliet, choose to die together.

What is this idealism that is so strong that it chooses death and the hope of another world rather than accept a less perfect life on this earth? What is it in this suffering that attracts us so powerfully that we always return to the flame, no matter how many times we are burned? This is what we ask as we look at the suffering and death of Tristan and Iseult.

On his wedding night, the ring of green jasper falls from Tristan's finger and clatters on the stones. That moment is the final great turning point in Tristan's life. He decides that, in order to be true to the inner ideal represented by Iseult the Fair, he must reject his wife. "And now what pity I feel for my wife, for her trust and her simple heart. See how these two Iseults have met me in an evil hour! and to each I have broken faith!"

In that moment an iron door shuts on half of Tristan's nature. Tristan decides to refuse his wife, and in the same act he gives up life itself. From that moment to his final day, he seems only to wait for the death that he believes will unite him, at last, with his ideal, his dream, his vision of perfection, his soul—all incarnated in Iseult the Fair.

He gives up all earthly love with Iseult of the White Hands; he will serve only the divine love, and he looks for his soul in the Queen. But Tristan and Iseult do not find their souls in each other. Ultimately they find in each other only a tormenting reflection of the divine realm that they hope to find on the other side of the grave. Tristan is doubly unhappy, for he has lost both Iseults. He has lost the enjoyment of earthly life with his wife, and by refusing to make a nonphysical relationship to Iseult the Fair, he has also lost his relationship with her. He can not have her in the way he demands. He has lost his inner life, and he despairs of ever finding it except by dying and meeting Iseult the Fair in heaven.

Had we looked, we could have seen Death approaching very early. The two lovers were already calling to Him when they stood beneath the tall pine-tree, longing for a perfect place where they could live their romantic vision. We could hear the longing in Tristan's voice as he spoke of the "other world":

> "But one day, friend, we shall go together to a fortunate land from which none returns. There, rises a castle of white marble; at each of its thousand windows burns a lighted candle; at each a minstrel plays and sings a melody without end . . ."

And hear again the words of Tristan as he stands before the King playing the fool, asking for the Queen. Where will he take her?

> "Oh! very high, between the clouds and heaven, into a fair chamber glazed. The beams of the sun shine through it, yet the winds do not trouble it at all. There would I bear the Queen in to that crystal chamber of mine, all compact of roses and the morning."

Where can such a beautiful land exist? How can we find our way there? Tristan plans to make the journey there by the dark path of death. As he takes leave of the Queen for the last time, he makes his appointment with her, their mutual appointment with death. He utters the prophecy that reveals his intention: "My death is near, and far from you my death will come of desire."

And Iseult answers:

> "O friend, fold your arms round me and strain me so that our hearts may break and our souls go free at last. Take me to that happy place of which you told me long ago. The fields whence none return, but where great singers sing their songs for ever. . . ."
>
> "I will take you to the Happy Palace of the living, Queen!" Tristan says. "The time is near. When it is finished, if I call you, will you come, my friend?"

Finally, when Tristan lies poisoned by the spear, he puts the ring of green jasper into Kaherdin's hand and sends him to Iseult with this message: "Say she must come, for we drank our death together."

Indeed, they drank their death together, and as the end approaches, death seems to be the object of all their longing. Their despair on earth is made bearable only by the perfection, beauty, and happiness of the world to come. But what is this glorious land of white marble castles and rosy chambers, this "Happy Palace of the living"?

This perfect and beautiful realm can only be the inner world. We all instinctively know of this world; we resonate with these lovers' words; their longing sets up a sympathetic vibration in our souls. It is the fairy-tale land, the world of imagination where the soul holds secret court with the gods. But why is this inner world of soul symbolized by Death? Why do Tristan and Iseult believe that they can only go there by the pathways of the dead?

From primordial times death has been conceived as a "going free" from the limited physical realm of time and space into the unlimited and measureless universe of spirit and eternity. This "liberation" from the physical is, for the unconscious, a symbol of something yet more subtle: the liberation of ego from the bounds of its tiny world and its petty viewpoint, into the vast, unbound, inner universe of psyche. Freed from literalism, death is not the end, but a symbol of profound change, of transformation.

The "land of death" is the inner world of the soul. The deepest meaning of death, experienced in the depths of the unconscious, is as symbol of transformation: the transformation of the ego that enters into the realm of the psyche, meets and joins with the soul, and consents to give up its tiny empire in order to live in the immensity of the greater universe.

To understand this opens a whole new vista for us: It is *transformation* that is required of us—not death! This is what is symbolized over and over in the great tales of romance, using "death" as symbol. This is the one solution to the conflicts, the confused loyalties, and the terrible sufferings of romance. The only true resolution is a change of consciousness and a change of values.

Even so, a real "death" awaits us within the transformative experience: It is the death of ego. By "death of ego" we do not mean that the ego evaporates or disappears. We mean that the ego makes a sacrifice of its old world, its old point of view, its old, ingrained attitudes. When a new set of values come into life and a new synthesis becomes possible, it must destroy the old world order of ego: Ego can only feel it as "death."

If ego takes this death as a threat, then it resists and fights the change. We all do this in romantic love; even when we see that we need to transform our values in order to experience the true revelation in romantic love, we still feel threatened: We still cling to our old attitudes, impose the same old demands on other people, and try to live out our fantasies of romance on the same old levels. To change, to question our own opinions, to alter our patterns, feels like impending disaster. This is the "death of the ego," the death that awaits us within transformation.

In Tristan's day, they took the symbol literally: They believed that they would only find the world of soul and spirit by dying, by leaving this physical body. Yet in one way they were wiser than we: They were more conscious of, and more direct about, what they sought in romantic love. The Cathars and troubadours flatly stated that they were seeking the transformation, that they were seeking it through passionate love and through death. Death, because it released them from the slavery of the flesh. Passion, because, in its otherworldly intensity, in both its ecstasy and its suffering, they saw a foretaste of the divine world. Romantic love was for them an *initiation.* The passion of love was thought to spiritualize the elect in anticipation of the final passion; it incinerated the human life that separates us from "the fields whence none return."

We are not so direct; we are unconscious of what we seek. But we have inherited the same beliefs. We walk through life longing for a transfiguring experience, the vision that will give our lives meaning and wholeness: We are searching for our souls, searching for the divine world. But we don't know how to experience the gods inwardly, on the symbolic level. Unconsciously, impulsively, like men and women possessed, we seek it in passion, falling in love, delivering ourselves over to a power that envelopes us and possesses us. It is ecstasy, it is suffering, it is a kind of death, but most of all it is a taste of what used to be sought in the afterlife: transfiguration. It is death and rebirth: One is dead to the world and alive to a realm that is bigger than life. As long as the passion lasts, so long as the projection can be maintained, this is what one feels. And this, above all, is what one seeks.

Tristan believes there are two ways he can touch the

inner world: first, through the suffering and ecstasy of his passion for Iseult the Fair; second, by literal death, by leaving this physical world. We modern Westerners have reduced the options still more; most of us seek the inner world in only one place—romantic passion. Why is this?

Partly, it is our Western dualism, the division of life in two: physical life on earth, spiritual life in the sky. Both Catharism and medieval Christianity teach Tristan that earth is nothing, that the spiritual life can only be found in the afterlife, in "heaven." This belief has become, in our minds, the unconscious idea that the spiritual side of life is always "somewhere else" or "over there." It is always somewhere other than where I am, someplace other than within my own life. We Westerners don't really believe that we can experience our gods and our spiritual life as an inner experience while pursuing our ordinary daily lives on earth. It is hard for us to think of the two worlds, inner and outer, coexisting simultaneously in one human being. This is why we always try to embody the divine world in something or someone outside ourselves.

Another reason for seeking our inner world in romantic love is simply that Westerners don't believe in the inner world; therefore, whatever we do with that unlived side of ourselves has to be unconscious, has to be projected out into the physical world. The fact of a nonphysical inner world is a difficult idea for Western people. We talk about inward realities, we talk of "soul" and "spirit," but we don't really believe in them. Over the centuries we have lost contact with the inner life and with its symbolism as our culture has turned ever more literal and materialist. In this area, we have actually done a reverse evolution.

In Tristan's time most men thought of "soul" and "spirit" as quasiphysical entities, only slightly more subtle than the physical body; they had to be located in a literal physical body or in a "place"—a "limbo" or a "heaven." They thought of heaven as a literal physical place, rather than a state of being, and actually spent centuries speculating over heaven's location in the physical universe!

Even several centuries after Tristan, in Galileo's day, the profession of astonomer was very dangerous because most people were convinced that the divine world was located "out there" among the stars and planets. Galileo was branded a heretic because he saw something through his telescope that contradicted that idea.

We haven't evolved much further in our own century. Our religion is romance: We locate the divine world in physical people—the people with whom we fall in love. And any psychologist who asserts (after consulting his telescope) that the divine world can't really be found in romance is likely to make people angry and be branded a spoilsport, if not a heretic.

Now we have found the secret cipher that decodes "suffering and death." We begin to see that the "death" we seek in romantic love is transformation, the end of the old world, the searing touch of the fire that slays and gives new life in the same instant. The suffering of romance is ultimately no different than the suffering of mysticism and religion: It is the pain shared by all mortals who would give birth to the divine world within their own lives, within this physical life and its finite limits.

> Why is it that we delight most of all in some tale of impossible love? Because we long for the *branding;* because we long to grow *aware* of what is on fire inside us. Suffering and understanding are deeply connected; death and self-awareness are in league; and European romanticism may be compared to a man to whom sufferings, and especially the

sufferings of love, are a privileged mode of understanding. (de Rougemont, *Love in the Western World,* pp. 51–52).

Suffering is the inevitable path that must be trod on the way to consciousness, the inevitable price for the transformation we seek. By no means can we escape it; we who try to evade it never succeed; and we are twice unlucky, for we pay the price, anyway, but miss our transformation. There is a terrible and immutable law at work: We only transform when we take our suffering consciously and voluntarily; to attempt to evade only puts us into the karmic cycles that repeat endlessly and produce nothing.

This, then, is why we suffer, and this is why, unconsciously, we even seek to suffer: "Because we long for the branding; because we long to grow aware of what is on fire inside us."

But freedom is given to us to choose how to take our suffering. Most people take it unconsciously. This is why suffering usually seems to lead nowhere, to produce only pain; this is why romance often seems to be a meaningless cycle: We fall in love, we set up our ideal of perfection, and in time, we are bitterly disappointed. We suffer. We follow our projections about, always searching for the one who will match the impossible ideal and will magically give us our transformation. And when we don't find the divine world where we search—in a human being—we suffer; we fall into despair.

But if we take our suffering consciously, voluntarily, then it gives us something in return; it produces the true transformation. To suffer consciously means to live through the "death of ego," to voluntarily withdraw one's projections from other people, to stop searching for the "divine world" in one's spouse, and instead to find one's own inner life as a psychological and religious act. It means to take responsibility for discovering one's own totality, one's own unconscious possibilities. It means to questions one's old patterns—to be willing to change. All of this involves conflict, self-questioning, uncovering duplicities one would rather not face. It is painful and difficult.

But this suffering leads us to our totality. It elevates romance into a path to the divine world. We discover that we don't have to die physically to find that world, but we do have to die symbolically: Our suffering is our symbolic death.

The wonder that is finally revealed is that we can live in the divine world even while we live in the flesh, here on this earth. For deep within each of us rises a "castle of white marble; at each of its thousand windows burns a lighted candle; at each a minstrel plays and sings a melody without end." To find that wondrous palace we must look neither to another person nor to the other side of the grave, but within ourselves.

If we live this death correctly—as paradoxical as this sounds—it becomes a journey of discovery leading toward a new life. Death is revealed as the other face of life. And the "death" that awaits at the very center of romance is not the destruction of life but the flowering of an inner world.

16

Iseult-Maya: The Dance of Illusion

At its best, romantic love is the high road to a double revelation: It leads us past the literalism and materialism of the Western mind and brings us face to face with the symbolic life; it opens our eyes to the meaning of human love. But at its worst, romantic love becomes a cycle of illusion that wastes our lives and distorts our loves instead of aiding them.

This two-edgedness of romantic love, which serves us if we live it correctly but destroys us if we don't, reflects the two-sidedness of anima: She can be Iseult, Queen of the Inner World, who leads us to our deepest inner selves, or she can be Maya, the Goddess of Illusion. In one role she serves life and gives it meaning; but her other face is terrible—she rips to shreds the fabric of ordinary life, she beguiles us away from all reality and turns our attempts at love into a perpetual dance of illusion. We have just seen Tristan and Iseult in that dance of anima, dancing steps we all know well.

It is time to remember how Jung spoke of the two faces of Iseult:

> The withdrawal of projections makes the anima what she originally was: an archetypal image which, in its right place, functions to the advantage of the individual. Interposed between the ego and the world, she acts like an ever-

> changing Shakti, who weaves the veil of Maya and dances the illusion of existence. But, functioning between the ego and the Unconscious, the anima becomes the matrix of all the divine and semi-divine figures, from the pagan goddess to the virgin, from the messenger of the Holy Grail to the saint. (Jung, *Psychology of the Transference*, par. 504)

Placed between my ego and the unconscious, my soul opens the way to God; she makes a spiritual life possible for me. Imported into my personal relations with people, she turns them into illusion; she casts the spell of Maya.

In Hindu myth Maya is the goddess who dances the dance of illusion, weaving a gossamer veil that hangs between humanity and reality, distorting our vision of what is. Often it is said that the purpose of yogic practice is to "see through the veil of Maya."

As our myth nears its end, that veil slips over Tristan's eyes. Maya casts her spell over him. It is no longer Iseult inspiring him, but Maya, keeping him in a perpetual dream. His feet never touch the ground; he sighs, he longs, he wanders back and forth between Carhaix and Cornwall in a delirium, a virtual madness. Nothing touches him, nothing interests him, except the image of Iseult that he carries in his mind. Her image obsesses him, but it no longer serves life: It leads toward nothing. He is lost in a fantasy that brings him no closer to the inner world yet cuts him off from the outer world of his friends, his wife, his physical life. For the rest of his days he wanders in Maya's dream, dead to all else, dancing distractedly to music that he alone hears, from a realm no one else can see.

Maya is Illusion: the distortion of reality, the loss of reality. Our story tells us that romantic love is afflicted with illusion; a man wakes up to his illusion when it suddenly dawns on him that the woman he is in love with will not, cannot, solve all his problems and make his life blissful with no further effort on his part. His wife awakens to her illusion when she sees that he is someone different from the man she thought she was marrying—and worse, that he is often insensitive and thoughtless, just like all other men. She hadn't seen the man; she'd seen her illusion. But where do these illusions come from?

Many Hindus, like some Christians, believe that the physical world around us is the illusory world—that only the spiritual world is real. Most Westerners, though, believe that the inner spiritual world is the illusion, that only the physical world is real. But illusion is neither the inner world of psyche nor the external physical world. Illusion is a distorted relationship between inner and outer. We give birth to illusion by superimposing our inner world of images—our continuous stream of fantasy—on the external world and on the people who live there. We see the physical world colored and distorted through the film of our inner images. Thus, as said Saint Paul: "Now we see as through a glass, darkly."

The physical world is true and real; the inner world is also true and real. It is when we muddle them, when we fail to live the inner world as symbol, when we try to locate it in literal people, that the illusory world is created. The illusory world is the projected world, which so distorts both inner and outer that we can see neither as it is.

When a man experiences a fantasy of ultimate peace and wholeness, he needs to understand his fantasy as a statement of what he can achieve within himself. But usually he will project his image of paradise on a woman, unconsciously asking her to fulfill it, to bring it into some physical actuality, to deliver it to him. In that instant he creates the illusion; he sees "through a glass, darkly." He no longer sees his external wife as she is, and he doesn't yet see his inner vision as the reality that it is. Both worlds are mangled; both worlds are dishonored.

Anima becomes Maya, not because there is something wrong with anima, but because of what men do with her. Let us remember that what we call anima is a man's soul. My soul is not some amorphous, sentimental notion invented for love letters. My soul is a specific part of me with a specific function: It is a psychological organ that performs a life-giving role within this strange and wonderful combination of psychological and physical parts that makes up a human being.

The soul of a human being is designed, in a sense, to enable him or her to see a different side of the cosmos, to experience a life and a perspective that is wide and vast. The soul can only do what it is designed to do, what is in its nature: It can only lead us toward the infinite. If we put our soul into finite situations, it keeps leading us toward the infinite; if we put our soul into personal situations it keeps pulling us toward the impersonal and the transpersonal. This is how Iseult becomes Maya—it is not because there is mischief in the soul but because the soul is so good, so persistent, in pulling us toward its side of existence, the side that resonates with infinity.

When a man invests his soul into his personal situations, she goes on doing what she must do: She pulls the personal situation toward the archetypal. She "infinitizes" his finite situation; she converts it into an allegory of great archetypal themes, eternal questions, holy quests and crusades. We see men put their souls into all sorts of finite human situations; we say that he is "blowing it all out of proportion" or "making a federal case of it" or "making a mountain out of a molehill." In such earthy ways we speak of "inflation"—the swelling-up of a finite situation because a man put his soul into it, and she, in accord with her nature, infinitized it. Thus Iseult becomes

Maya, anima is changed into the inadvertent author of illusion.

Anima's nature is to create the fantasy side of life. When we experience her fantasy consciously on the symbolic level, she creates a world of splendor, a view of the timeless universe that lifts us out of the bounds of personal life and acquaints us with what is universal and eternal. We see ourselves and our lives in a different perspective, we see ourselves in the flow of the ages, and we see that our lives are individual manifestations of what has always been and will always be.

My soul is that part of me that strives always to renew my awareness of what is universal, of the great motifs in life that are outside all personal matters and transcend all personal lives yet are common to all. Our souls are pointed toward God, like sunflowers that only face the light; they see only the archetypes, the inner gods, the great leitmotifs behind all individual existences. This is why anima puts such a strain on personal life: Anima is not interested in the individual idiosyncrasies of my personal daily life—whether my bank account is balanced, whether my relationships with people are clear, whether the lawn is mowed. Her eyes are on the cosmic accounts, balanced in the scales of Libra, where the only issue is my inner wholeness. Her values are not human values but cosmic values; her only interest is whether I live and experience every great theme of human existence that is contained in potential within my being.

Each man's soul demands that he be, and that he live, every great archetypal role in the collective unconscious: the betrayer and the betrayed, the lover and the beloved, the oppressor and the victim, the noble and the ignoble, the conquerer and the conquered, the warrior and the priest, the man of sorrows and the self reborn.

When a man tries to live his soul within his finite

marriage with a woman, his soul puffs up and distorts his view of both wife and marriage. His soul keeps trying to pull the relationship toward the infinite, make it into an allegory of love, death, and paradise lost, convert this human marriage into a huge, sweeping archetypal drama. That drama goes on inside him, anyway, all the time—at the fantasy level. If he could learn to keep it there, to see it as symbol and experience it as symbol, then he could live correctly with his soul. He could follow his soul in his inner life toward the infinite but stay within the limits of the finite in his relationship with his wife.

In his dream work, his active imagination, his meditation, he would follow his soul off to Camelot and joust with the knights. He would quest for the Holy Grail, fight with dragons and Morholts, rescue maidens, heal the sick and find healing for his own wounds. He would betray and be betrayed, he would sin and repent, he would take revenge: He would live out all the archetypes in the collective unconscious, but in symbolic form. He would keep the infinite contained in symbol—the one vessel that can hold it without cracking and without destroying his personal life.

From a symbolic journey toward the infinite, following his soul in imagination and dream, a man could find his way back to the finite world. There he would find his home, his wife, his relationship intact. There he would consent to deal with the finite questions and limits of ordinary life. He could learn not to fight with his wife because he is angry with characteristics within himself, or because his soul wants to lead him to battle with inner villains. He would learn to see his fantasy as his own inner event, and to experience it on that interior level.

A man who puts anima into his marriage is putting his fantasy into his marriage and turning it into a series of archetypal scenes, a playground for the impersonal forces of the unconscious. His wife, if she is not joining the fantasy, begins to realize that she is not so much a wife as the supporting cast in a gigantic stage play: the cosmic drama that goes on forever in her husband's inner world.

> Anima as function of relationship is far indeed from relatedness. It seems odd that anima could ever have been considered as a help in human relationship. In each of her classical shapes she is a non-human or half-human creature, and her effects leads us away from the individually human situation. She makes moods, distortions, illusions, which serve human relatedness only where the persons concerned share the same mood or fantasy. If we want "to relate," then anima begone! Nothing disturbs more the accurate feeling between persons than anima. . . .
>
> The relatedness of George and Mary depends upon the specific natures of George and Mary. Their relatedness reflects their living process of feeling, and their relationship is unique to them. If their relationship were anima-determined, it would become a reflection less of them, and more of an archetypal fantasy playing through them. Then they become collective actors performing an unconscious fantasy, i.e., lovers, quarrelers, cohorts. . . .
>
> . . . She does not lead into human feeling, but out of it. As the function that relates conscious and unconscious, she occludes conscious feeling, making it unconscious and making the human, inhuman. She puts other things in mind than the human world. (Hillman, "Anima," pp. 111–12)

In the instant that a man falls "in love," he goes beyond love itself and begins the worship of his soul-in-woman. Anima immediately begins to blow his human relationship out of human proportion. Love is not just love but a divine ecstasy; every sight of the beloved brings, not a quiet happiness, but unearthly bliss. But then, as soul swings her vision to the negative side of the archetypes, every mood becomes the occasion for a fight or a separation, every slight is the ultimate betrayal, every glance at another man or woman justifies blasts of anger and jealousy: Every ordinary event becomes part of a huge drama. Anima can only lead men away from finite ordinariness and into that universal play.

Strangely, this is the point where a man feels most unique, most individual, as though this has never happened to anyone other than him and his beloved. In fact, it is at this point that he *loses* his individuality. The lovers lose their individual identities; they are Tristan and Iseult or Romeo and Juliet—actors in a collective play where the script is predetermined and the scenes are known beforehand. It is precisely because one has ceased to be oneself and has become a player in a universal drama, that one feels so intense, so out of the ordinary, and at first, so wonderful.

But, like Semele, who demanded of Zeus that he appear to her in all the power of his godhead, human relationships simply incinerate—"burn out"—when they are subjected to the impersonal, divine power contained in the anima and animus projections. People often say that they are "burned out" by a relationship. It is literally true. They are so exhausted by the sheer intensity of romantic love as we try to live it, by the ecstasies and battles, the partings and reconciliations, that there is finally nothing left—neither life force nor goodwill nor affection—with which to love and companion someone on a human level.

It is no wonder that many people, finding themselves caught in the dance of illusion, become embittered. They decide that romantic love is a treadmill, a meaningless sham, and they give up on love. But there is a better way to leave the dance. One needs to graduate out of the dance by finding the truth that is masked by the illusion. If we look diligently for that hidden truth, we come full circle: We find ourselves back on the bark with Tristan,

Iseult, and the love potion. We are asking once again why the splendor of God comes to us, not through our religious lives, but in our loves, our projections, our illusions. The answer is startling: It is because we do not have religious lives, and the divine realm has to find us, even trap us, where it can. We have churches, we have dogma, we have doctrine, we have opinions, we have groups and meetings; but we do not have religious lives because we pay little attention to our souls or to our inner lives.

Tristan shows us ourselves. Tristan never seeks Iseult the Fair consciously to follow her to a spiritual life; he never gives any voluntary heed to his soul. But his soul finds him, against his will, in the love potion and then in the Dance of Illusion. We, also, have paid no heed to our souls. We have not sought our souls and our gods consciously or voluntarily, but our souls have found us and snared us through our projections—our illusions. A man drinks the potion; he stares at Iseult, seeing not Iseult but Maya; and imperceptibly, without his knowledge, his feet move and he joins the dance.

If a man would evolve out of illusion and pull the illusion out of his loves, there is one direct act of the will required. Merely to decide to give up his projections as a heroic discipline won't work; he can only pull anima out of his marriage, relationships, and personal lives when he has affirmatively provided a place for her on another level in his life.

The inner act required of a Western man is to affirm his own religious nature. It means to affirm seriously that the images and feelings that flow out of him in dream, fantasy, and imagination are the stuff of the divine realm, a separate order of reality distinct from his physical and personal life but equally real and equally important. He must be willing to take those images seriously, to spend time living with them, to see them as powers of great importance within himself, inhabitants of a spiritual realm that his soul transmits to him in symbol.

One may do this by traditional religious practice, by contemplative meditation, by yoga, by fantasy and dream work, or by Jung's active imagination. But it requires an inner practice, an affirmative soul-life, actually lived day by day.

If a man does this he begins to learn the difference between inner and outer, between what must be lived symbolically and what must be lived physically. He projects, but he learns what to do with projection; he is not overwhelmed and determined by his projections. He suffers, but his suffering produces something: evolution and change rather than vain repetition of the dance. His soul, permitted at last to live and infinitize in Her natural element—symbol—moves less and less into his personal, finite life. She no longer needs to snare him by inflating his human love, his relationship, or his marriage.

This is a differentiation, an evolution, and a consciousness that comes to the man who will pay the price. For him, the dance quietly fades, changed into the symbolic life that it masked; Maya lifts her veil, and his vision clears. He learns what it is to be mortal man with an immortal soul.

Conclusion

17

The White Bison Spirit Woman

The genius of the story of Tristan and Iseult is that it tells us exactly what is. It shows us in amazing detail what has happened to us as a culture and as individuals. Like a faithful mirror, it reflects back to us our attitudes and our behavior and it shows the psychological forces at work in us.

But the myth leaves us, in a sense, in a quandary. It tells us what is, but it doesn't tell us what to do about it.

Just as myth enables us to see ourselves as we are, so myth and dream will often give us the prescription for the problem. We will now look at two other mythical statements that seem to offer us a solution to our dilemma.

The first is a myth of the Oglala Sioux nation, recounted by the great medicine man Black Elk—the story of the White Bison Spirit Woman. This is the story of how a divine woman brought the first sacred medicine pipe to the Oglala people.

> A very long time ago, they say, two scouts were out looking for bison; when they came to the top of a high hill and looked north, they saw something coming a long way off, and when it came closer they cried out, "It is a woman!" and it was. Then one of the scouts, being foolish, had bad thoughts and spoke them; but the other said: "That is a sacred woman; throw all bad thoughts away."
>
> When she came still closer, they saw that she wore a fine

white buckskin dress, that her hair was very long and that she was young and very beautiful. And she knew their thoughts and said in a voice that was like singing: "You do not know me, but if you want to do as you think, you may come." And the foolish one went; but just as he stood before her, there was a white cloud that came and covered them. And the beautiful young woman came out of the cloud, and when it blew away the foolish man was a skeleton covered with worms.

Then the woman spoke to the one who was not foolish: "You shall go home and tell your people that I am coming and that a big tepee shall be built for me in the center of the nation." And the man, who was very much afraid, went quickly and told the people, who did at once as they were told; and there around the big tepee they waited for the sacred woman. And after a while she came, very beautiful and singing, and as she went into the tepee this is what she sang:

With visible breath I am walking.
A voice I am sending as I walk.
In a sacred manner I am walking.
With visible tracks I am walking.
In a sacred manner I walk.

And as she sang, there came from her mouth a white cloud that was good to smell. Then she gave something to the chief, and it was a pipe with a bison calf carved on one side to mean the earth that bears and feeds us, and with twelve eagle feathers hanging from the stem to mean the sky and the twelve moons, and these were tied with a grass that never breaks. "Behold!" she said. "With this you shall multiply and be a good nation. Nothing but good shall come from it. Only the hands of the good shall take care of it and the bad shall not even see it." Then she sang again and went out of the tepee; and as the people watched her going, suddenly it was a white bison galloping away and snorting, and soon it was gone.

> This they tell, and whether it happened so or not I do not know; but if you think about it, you can see that it is true. (Black Elk, in Neihardt, *Black Elk Speaks*, pp. 3–4)

Here, in mythical language, we have the essence of what we have been trying to say. Here, in the contrast between a wise scout and a foolish scout, we see the two approaches that man may take to anima, and the results that flow from each way. We cannot avoid her, for she comes to us as we stand on the hunting grounds, going about our ordinary life, little expecting a visitor from the "other world." But how we treat her makes the difference between blessedness and destruction.

Anima is a sacred woman. Our willingness, or unwillingness, to treat her as a sacred being is what makes the difference. This inner feminine that we project is "Spirit Woman," like unto White Bison Woman, a being of the other world. If we are like the wise scout, we say: "That is a sacred woman; throw away all bad thoughts!" And when we treat her as a sacred being, then she brings the medicine pipe, she brings the sky and the twelve moons, she brings us our means of knowing the other world.

If we are like the foolish scout, if we try to make her into a physical being by projecting her onto an external person, then we lose her sacredness. We lose the chance to receive her gift. The terrible thing about anima is that she lets us approach her as we will—foolishly, or wisely. She says: "You do not know me, but if you want to do as you think, you may come." But the price is terrible! The price for failing to treat her as a sacred being, as a spirit creature of the inner world, is not only the loss of the other world but the destruction of human life while we live it. This is the meaning of this worm-eaten skeleton of the foolish scout lying in the dirt at her feet.

When we approach anima as a divine presence in the

inner world, what blessings she bestows! The gift she brings is the sacred world, the restoration of the sacred in our lives.

So much of our lives is spent in a longing and a search—for what, we do not know. So many of our ostensible "goals," so many of the things we think we want, turn out to be the masks behind which our real desires hide; they are symbols for the actual values and qualities for which we hunger. They are not reducible to physical or material things, not even to a physical person; they are psychological qualities: love, truth, honesty, loyalty, purpose—something we can feel is noble, precious, and worthy of our devotion. We try to reduce all this to something physical—a house, a car, a better job, or a human being—but it doesn't work. Without realizing it, we are searching for the *Sacred.* And the sacred is not reducible to anything else.

Sacredness is, in a sense, a feeling—but a feeling that goes to the very heart of life. It is the feeling of recognition directed toward what is great and high enough to give our small lives meaning, to put our personal journeys in a greater perspective. It is the feeling of reverence. What we call the sacred is ultimately a universe of meaning against which we measure our personal efforts, our personal lives, to see whether they, too, have meaning.

For the male psyche, the discovery of the sacred, the communion with the sacred, is always through the inner feminine. It is White Bison Woman who brings the sacredness in life, the vision of the sky and the twelve moons.

With visible breath I am walking.
A voice I am sending as I walk.
In a sacred manner I am walking.

With visible tracks I am walking.
In a sacred manner I walk.

Like a river of being in which all the streams of inner life run together, all the values that we feel instinctively as "sacred" converge in the image of anima and are made conscious in us through her. She is, as Jung said: "the matrix of all the divine and semi-divine figures, from the pagan goddess to the virgin, from the messenger of the Holy Grail to the saint."

We seem never to go searching directly or consciously for the sacred side of life. Like the two scouts, we wander in our old hunting grounds, seeking only the habitual and the known. Suddenly we are confronted with an unknown part of ourselves. She comes walking a long way off, arrayed in white buckskin; and when she speaks, it is a voice like singing. At first we are confused: She bears the image of woman, and we want to believe that we can relate to her as to a woman. It is hard to believe that she is not physical woman, but a metaphysical force so powerful that we dare not try to touch her physically.

This is the fact that the sacred presents to us: This is how the sacred becomes one "person" and speaks to us with a single voice. This is anima.

Otherwise we would feel the sacred only vaguely as the "other side of life," the "other side of myself," that we have never touched, never known. It manifests as dreams of adventures we long for, triumphs we can almost taste, luminous men and women we meet walking in the corridors and fabled kingdoms of our minds. Without reasoning, without thinking, our feelings pull us toward the other side of ourselves, where every image vibrates with the promise of an extraordinary meaning, experience, or sense of wholeness.

All this converges and focuses in one inner being;

White Bison Woman comes to the two scouts as a stranger from a larger world outside the ego's vision, the ego's opinions or notions of "reality." Her reality is so much larger, so filled with potential for enlarging our lives and for giving them meaning, that the unconscious says to us: "This is sacred; this is what you must treat as sacred."

White Bison Woman sings: "With visible breath I am walking. A voice I am sending as I walk."

Breath is the age-old symbol of life and spirit. For ancient people breath was the very substance of God, breathed into our nostrils by our creator, a spark of the divine energy lent to mortal flesh for a handsbreadth of time on this earth: the breath of life. As White Bison Woman walks with "visible" breath, she makes what we call the "spiritual" side of life visible, manifest. She makes the invisible, visible.

When we treat White Bison Woman as our soul, she has the power to make the "sacred" into an immediate, direct, conscious, experience. "With visible tracks I am walking," she says. She is not physical; she is Psyche, Pneuma, Light-as-wind, yet her tracks may be seen. She has substance; she is the power that gives the sacred world the substance of symbol. She takes it off the level of the theoretical, the abstract, the sentimental, the figure-of-speech. She renders the sacred accessible in the here-and-now: touched, felt, and experienced as though it were physical. The spirit world is made immediate and palpable through symbolic experience.

Thus, she has the power to give us psychological faith:

> . . . The faith arising from the psyche which shows as faith in the reality of the soul. Since psyche is primarily image

> and image always psyche, this faith manifests itself in the belief in images. . . . Psychological faith begins in the *love of images,* and it flows mainly through the shapes of persons in reveries, fantasies, reflections and imaginations. Their increasing vivification gives one an increasing conviction of having, and then of being, an interior reality of deep significance transcending one's personal life.
>
> Psychological faith is reflected in an ego that gives credit to images and turns to them in its darkness. (Hillman, *Revisioning Psychology,* p. 50)

We may come to see that psychological faith and spiritual faith intersect at the deepest level, for the early Christians knew that "faith is the substance of things hoped for, the evidence of things unseen"—and we find that it is in the numinous symbols, flowing through the soul to the conscious mind, that we apperceive the substance of what we hope, the substance of what we dream, the substance of what lives within us beyond the limits of this physical sphere.

It is anima—White Bison Woman—who brings to the conscious mind the evidence of realities not seen in the physical world. We seek the spirit realm in romantic love, we seek it in sex, we seek it in physical possessions and drugs and physical people; but it is not there. It is only revealed through the soul.

The medicine pipe is the power to contact the "other world." This power consists in the *conscious use of symbolism,* for it is by symbolic experience that we breathe in the gods of the archetypal worlds like smoke from the sacred pipe.

By the twelve eagle feathers, representing the sky and the twelve moons, we receive the power to know the totality of life, a vision which merges spirit and matter, sacredness and ordinariness. Twelve is the number that symbolically combines the three and the four. We have spoken of three and four earlier: Three symbolizes the ordered, limited, finite life of the physical world and practical, daily existence. Four symbolizes the infinite realm of the soul where one is lifted into a vision of the limitless archetypal realm and the wholeness of the cosmos. Twelve combines these two sides of human nature in a synthesis. Twelve combines heaven and earth, the "other world" with the ordinary world, the spiritual life with the physical life. This is the symbolism of the twelve disciples who surround Christ in a perfect circle in the Christian mandala, the twelve moons of the solar year, and the twelve signs of the zodiac that mark off the revolving ages of the galactic universe.

On the other side of the medicine pipe is carved a bison calf, telling us that the earth, and our earthly human life, is also drawn into this synthesis with the sacred when we approach the Lady wisely.

Perhaps the deepest lesson we learn from the wise scout is this: The quality of sacredness consists not only in what is there in the inner world, but also in the attitude we take toward it. It is made up not only of what is, but also of what one does with it. It is up to us to recognize it, to treat it as the sacred, in order to experience its power. The great power of White Bison Woman is manifested to the people only because the wise scout sees that she is sacred and gives her the respect that is her due.

For anima to bestow her gifts she depends on someone, an individual human ego, who will open his eyes and acknowledge her sacredness. If the wise scout had followed the path of the foolish man, there would be two skeletons lying in the dust, not one. The "other world" would still not be revealed to the nation; no great tepee would stand in the midst of the people; there would be no medicine pipe with which to call the Thunder Nation and seek its help.

Psychologically, the quality of sacredness consists in a double flow of energy: It is partly the revelation of the inner world to my ego, and it is partly my ego's reverence toward the inner world of archetypes. Only when my ego has a capacity for reverence, only when respect and awe flow from me, can anything be "sacred" for me.

Here is a strange and wonderful fact, which shows why people have always believed that the evolution of the cosmos is a partnership between God and humankind: The sacred is always there, closer to us than any physical person could be, but it takes on the power to fill our lives with meaning and quality only when we open our eyes and bow down in awe. This is one of the great mysteries: It is our consciousness, our act of recognition, that has the power to make things into what they are, and to make the sacred, sacred.

Most of us are more like the foolish scout: Our irreverent culture teaches us from childhood that nothing is holy, that nothing deserves our reverence, that everything in life can be reduced to either physical possession or a sex act. The wise scout knows he is confronted with something that is outside his experience, something he can't deal with by the ego's usual "bag of tricks." He senses her sacredness and he waits on her with reverence. He warns the foolish scout: "That is a sacred woman; throw all bad thoughts away."

What does the wise man mean when he says: "Throw all bad thoughts away?" What makes them "bad"? It is not because they are sexual thoughts. The American Indians, unlike us, did not have a tradition of puritanism; they did not denigrate the physical and the sexual. The problem is more subtle: The foolish scout is trying to find in the sexual side of life what can't be located there. He is trying to turn Spirit Woman into a physical being, trying to experience her through physical contact. In psychological terms, he is trying to make her physical by projecting her onto an external woman. The results are devastating: Instead of the benevolent Bison Goddess, he meets Kali, Goddess of Death, and she leaves his fleshless bones in the dust.

If there is such a thing as psychological blasphemy, it is to take what is sacred and try to convert it to something else; it is to try to make the sacred into grist for the ego's mill. Psychological sin does not consist in sex nor in being physical nor in "immorality" but rather in calling a thing other than what it really is, treating it as something other than what it is, pretending to do one thing while doing another. This is the sin against consciousness, the refusal to take life consciously. The foolish scout's thoughts are "bad" because he is confronted with what is spiritual, sacred, and transpersonal, and he wants to treat it as though it were physical, sexual, and personal. He wants to reduce White Bison Woman to an appendage of his ego world.

She instructs us: "You shall go home and tell your people that I am coming, and that a big tepee shall be built for me in the center of the nation."

To build her tepee in the midst of the nation means to make a place for anima, and a place for the sacred, in the very center of my life. It means to devote time and energy to experiencing my psyche, to exploring my own unconscious, to discovering who I am and what I am when I am not just this ego. The first thing required for a Western man is to acknowledge that the sacred world exists. He has to be willing to consider that behind his fantasy of the "perfect" woman, the "perfect" way of life, the "perfect" relationship, he is looking for something that is outside this world of phenomena: He is looking for the sacred. He has to spend time and energy learning to experience these energies, which manifest in symbol and fantasy, as inner realities, as inner parts of himself. This is what it means to take White Bison Woman as she is, as Spirit Woman, and to prepare for her a place at the center of the nation.

She comes walking with visible breath, with visible tracks, walking in a sacred manner. She will come to us if we prepare a sacred dwelling for her, if we will open our eyes and see her as she is. But her true dwelling is composed of the stuff of our own attitudes toward her, of our sense of reverence. The place we prepare is a place within; if she will dwell with us at all, it must be there.

18

The Dream of the Bell of the Holy Virgin

Some dreams are not for one man or woman alone; in their universal implications they are mythical utterances of the collective unconscious: They are dreams for the people. This is a dream that comes out of the Western collective unconscious, the dream of a man of this century, in his early thirties. It tells us how a modern Westerner may resolve his terrible struggles with anima and romantic love.

> I am carrying the bell that once belonged to the Virgin Mary to the great basilica which was built centuries ago to house it when it was found. The shape of the bell was known, and a niche has been prepared over the altar, exactly the correct size to fit the bell. A priest has been on duty at all times for several centuries to accept the bell when it would be returned. I walk into the basilica, down the long aisle, and present the bell to the waiting priest. Together we lift it up and hang it from the hook in its niche. The bell fits its place perfectly.
>
> The priest has been instructed to go to the west end of the basilica, when the Virgin's bell should be returned, and to ring the great bells in the towers to announce to the world that the bell had been found and returned to Christianity. Those great bells have never sounded in all the years of their life, but have waited until the day when the bell of the Virgin Mary would be returned. I sit on a bench

> by the side of the altar while the priest hurries the length of the basilica to ring the great bells.
>
> What should I do? Should I wait and claim all the fame and adulation that would come to me as the discoverer of the bell of the Virgin Mary? Or should I slip quietly away and avoid all the involvement? The priest, in his excitement, has not looked at me, so I could still claim anonymity. I decide on the latter.
>
> Just as the great bells begin to ring and the town's populace begins to rush toward the basilica, I slip out a side door and begin my solitary journey out of the city.

Here, in powerful and beautiful symbolic language, is an answer to the questions we are asking, an answer that comes from the very deep places of the unconscious and speaks to our modern problem. We are asking what modern Western man is to do with his soul. How does he extricate his soul from romantic love? How does he live with Iseult the Fair without destroying his relationship to Iseult of the White Hands? How can he give anima her place in his life but disentangle her from his human relationships? How can he learn to honor his soul without dishonoring woman?

It should not surprise us that we find part of our answer in a basilica, amid these great symbols of the religious life. We have been in the presence of the love potion, we have seen a white palace where a minstrel sings at each of a thousand windows and a sacred tepee set in the center of the nation—now the basilica. On the path we have trod, in the presence of powerful symbols of transformation, we begin to see clearly what at first was unthinkable: The path that leads to an understanding of romantic love also leads inevitably to our religious nature, to the spiritual side of our being that we have so zealously sidestepped.

We have learned that romantic love draws on a huge

power system in the unconscious, an energy so great that we can only speak of it in the language of religion and mysticism: We "adore," we "worship" our beloved; when we are in love we are "completed," we are "in heaven," we "die." Here is revealed the quest for godhead, Fire from Heaven, spiritual enlightenment, meaning, consciousness of self. In the West, as in no other culture in history, this huge force is routed, not into our religion or our mystical life, but into our human loves; romantic love has become the channel through which this awesome force flows into daily human life.

Now we are asking what we are to do with this awesome force. How can we channel it correctly so that it will enrich our lives—in the realms both of spirit and of relationship—rather than sabotage them.

This dream answers us in clear and vivid language: "Put the divine part of yourself back into the cathedral where it belongs and live the human part of yourself where it belongs—in ordinariness and simplicity." We must take our soul out of romantic love and return it to an inner place—the inner cathedral.

The weary traveler who trudges to the door of this great basilica is covered with the dust of a long journey, exhausted from the weight of a burden he has carried for centuries. This bell is too large and heavy to be carried by this single mortal man. It is too heavy to be carried in the personal ego life, too awesome to be put into his personal relationship with mortal woman. It is too great a burden to place on his marriage. They have already snapped under the weight. There is only one structure large enough and strong enough to hold this bell: It is the basilica.

Since the twelfth century, when the first Tristan took the bell out of the temple, drank the love potion, and began to try to contain this power within his love affairs,

Western man has struggled to carry the bell. He has tried to carry the bell within his personal life, his marriages, and his worldly empires. Now, nearly a thousand years later, he has forgotten that the bell had a divine origin. He has sacrificed the sacred to the secular, and psyche to ego for so long that he can't remember to whom the bell belongs. His back is nearly broken and he is weary unto death with the weight; his mortal human relationships are in a shambles from the crushing burdens he has placed on them, but he knows no other way. He doesn't remember the basilica; he doesn't know where it is.

This bell is our experience of anima; it is her voice. It reminds us of the words of White Bison Woman: "A voice I am sending as I walk." Like the bell, anima sends forth a voice for us to hear; she sings, and her song draws us into inner life. Her power is to give immediacy to the contents of our unconscious, to manifest the archetypes as living, breathing images whom we experience as forces living within us.

The bell represents lyrical knowledge of a man's psyche in the same sense that Hispanic people speak of *el modo lirico:* knowledge that comes of direct experience rather than of intellectual activity. The bells and music of Christendom have been the only voices by which the West told of the spirit without getting lost in concepts, abstractions, and words; the bells send forth a sound that is pure feeling, that darts past the mind and sets up an involuntary reverberation in the soul.

Anima, like the bell, has the power to reveal the Dionysian side of spiritual experience, where truth is *felt* with the senses, felt in the images that flow from the unconscious, felt as a living encounter with inner "persons." Indeed, the bells are among the few remnants of Dionysus in our Western religion; they call us to music, hymn, dance, feeling—to at-oneness with the cosmic drama of sacrifice and rebirth. The bells recall that King David danced before God.

The dream tells us that this bell does not belong to one's ego: It belongs, like the sacred pipe, to an inner "Nation," an inner "Christendom." It was known that something that belonged to all, that it was the church's duty to guard, would one day return to the basilica. In symbol this means that something that belonged in the arena of the spiritual life, outside the personal ego-life, that should have been guarded reverently in the inner world, has been lost. This is our soul; this is our psyche. Lost at first in the unconscious, it went wandering out into the ego world; through the love potion it was projected into personal human relationships. We tried to make the superpersonal into the personal; what belonged to the unconscious we tried to make a fief of the ego. But this power is destined to be given up by the ego, to be returned to the inner "cathedral."

It is difficult for us to imagine what it means to return a part of our lives to "the cathedral." It does not necessarily mean to become involved with an external, collective religion. It does mean to differentiate between what belongs in our external lives and what belongs to the inner self. It means to take something that we have been trying to live through our external relationships and live it, instead, in a quiet, private, inner place—a place that exists only on the level of spirit.

Deep within each of us is such a place, a crystal chamber "all compact of roses and the morning," a great basilica where true-voiced bells wait to announce the return of Soul from her wanderings. To return anima to the cathedral means for a man to sacrifice something on the level of his ego-life, to sacrifice his claim to live his soul by projection on woman. It means to take that burden off an external person and place it within the powerful inner edifice that was made to bear it.

Sometimes dreams are given us at a time when we must face a "death of ego"—a sacrifice of some level on which we have lived—to compensate our fears and our dismal expectations. Dreams give us a sense of proportion and lend us courage by showing us the beauty and glory of the thing we do, which we can't see for ourselves, and the splendor of the life that awaits us on the other side of our sacrifice.

To return anima to the basilica is a sacrificial act. All men have the option of trying to live anima through other people. To give up that attempt takes a conscious act of sacrifice; one must sacrifice a whole level of existence in order to move on to another. From the ego's viewpoint, it looks like death. To give up living anima by projection means to pull most of the artificial intensity out of relationships; it means that things will seem quieter and less exciting. To put his soul in the cathedral and stop trying to live it though a woman means that a man removes an entire dimension of his life from his human relationship and re-establishes it elsewhere, on another level of himself—a level that he can't live outwardly, that he must live by himself. To his ego it feels as though he is impoverishing his human relationship or cheating himself. At first he feels that half the thrills, excitement, fun, and intensity is taken out of human relationship. With time he learns that his soul-life never really belonged there and that his human relationship is actually thriving better without it; but for a time, it feels dismal.

This is the feeling that this bell-carrier has, the dreamer of the dream. If he gives the bell back, he feels as though he is giving up something in his personal, ego life. It is also the feeling the foolish Indian scout suffered when he was warned not to touch the Spirit Woman: He felt that he would be giving up something he wanted, something that excited and thrilled him on the ego level.

The symbolism of the great basilica, the pealing of the great bells that have waited all their lives for the return of the sacred bell, tells us of the glory and the beauty that waits on the other side of the sacrifice. By this imagery the dream tells us that our egos do not really lose anything by putting our souls where they belong, for the cathedral is inside us, it is part of us, and what seems to be lost to our egos is not lost but transformed into something on a greater level—something with the towering immensity of the basilica, with the ecstatic beauty of the voices of the great bells.

In fact, our ego empire has never truly insulated us against the mysteries or against the call of the basilica. As we have learned, the soul finds its way into our lives through one great open gap in the ego's armor: romantic love. This is why romantic love, this curious blend of the numinous and the deadly, has become the strongest single force in our culture: It has become, by default, the vessel in which we struggle to contain everything that has been excluded from our ego empires, everything of the unconscious—all that is numinous, unfathomable, awesome, all that inspires worship in us.

The dreamer of the dream came to understand this. The wise Indian scout understands it in the presence of White Bison Woman. He sees that he is in the presence of something of another world, and that he must not try to keep it for his ego but return it to the place that has been prepared for it, the one place that is powerful enough to contain it.

If Tristan had had this dream, if he had understood this dream, could he have done differently with the love potion? and with Iseult the Fair? Like the dreamer, he could have gone out the side door silently, anonymously.

He would have left that divine part of himself in the temple, put the human part of himself in human dimensions, and he would not have mixed the two. The whole burden of this dream is to learn to differentiate the two: the divine part and the ordinary, human, personal part.

Now, we have seen this as symbol. But in practice, how do we do it? How do we return this bell to the temple? How do we make a new home for this divine, overwhelming part of ourselves that we never asked for, but that we always find, tucked away under an arm or loaded on our backs like the bell?

Doctor Jung used to return a patient to his ancestral religion as quickly as possible if that person could do it. He would send a Catholic back to confessions and masses, a Jew back to the synagogue, a Parsee back to his native roots. If that way is open to a man or woman, it is the simplest and most direct way to return this divine part of ourselves to the basilica. But for many people this is not possible; the ritual and symbols of external, culturally transmitted religion no longer have life for them.

For such people—and there are more and more of them—there are other ways. One has to understand that the ultimate basilica, the ultimate cathedral, synagogue, or temple, is inside. What is required is not so much an external, collective religion, but an inner experience of the numinous, divine realm that is manifested through the psyche. For such people the religious life, the basilica, is found in the daily hours of solitary meditation, symbolic ritual, active imagination, interaction with images flowing through fantasy, ethical confrontation with the inner "persons" who reveal themselves in our dreams.

This is the symbolic life—taken voluntarily, consciously, with an attitude of reverence, with the same devotion and intensity that the medieval Christian mystics put into contemplative prayer or the Hindu puts into the vision of Shiva or the Zen Buddhist puts into Zazen. By such a life we find our way back to the primordial ground from which all religion grew: the individual dreams, visions, and vivid personal encounters with the persons of the inner world. Before ever there was dogma and doctrine there was Jacob wrestling with an angel, Paul struck down on the road to Damascus by a vision of Christ, Gautama seated beneath the Bodhi Tree, seized by the oneness of the universe.

There is an inner temple, but it looks more difficult to us and it seems more solitary: One feels like the man of the dream, who, having delivered the precious burden to the holy place, lets himself out a side door into a dusty road and walks off into anonymity as far as his personal life is concerned.

This is perhaps the most moving and powerful event in the dream: the decision of this modern Tristan, not only to give the bell back to the holy place, but to give up the power, the adulation, the drama, the ego-importance he could have had from having the bell in his personal possession. His exit through the side door is a true and correct sacrifice of ego, a genuine transformation. Unexpectedly, this event reveals to us that one of the root issues in romantic love is *humility:* the humility of an ego that is willing to give up inflating and puffing up its ego world, its personal relationships, into a dramatic power system. A deep humility is required to return that divine part of oneself to the cathedral.

Probably Tristan could have done no differently than he did. Western man has had to drink the love potion, he has had to find his way to anima and to the gods in the only way he knows. But with the centuries behind us, he has spent his time in the Forest of Morois; he has wandered far and carried a heavy burden along countless dusty roads. He has fallen in love, and out of love; he has betrayed and suffered betrayal; he has married Iseult of the White Hands, and yet he has wandered away in loneliness —always carrying the bell, always seeking Iseult the Fair in his loves, looking for her image in every face he sees. He has the right, now, to learn from the past, to learn from his experience, and to learn from his dreams.

If Tristan will learn today from this dream, he will make Iseult the Fair the queen of his inner world, the soul figure who will conduct him inwardly into the presence of the gods. He will take her to the inner temple and place her upon a throne of gold: It fits her, for it has awaited her for many centuries. He will cease trying to find her outside, in a mortal woman or in external circumstances. And after Tristan slips out the side door of the basilica, he will make his way quietly to a castle in Carhaix. There he will seek a chamber where his wife awaits him: Iseult of the White Hands. And as he takes her hand, he will discover a mystery: Iseult whom he left enthroned in a vast basilica has been restored to him, in a correct form and on a correct level; this simple, mortal woman, the Princess of Brittany, is also divine, and this chamber is a holy place.

19

Of Human Love

People become so wearied of the cycles and dead ends of romance that they begin to wonder if there is such a thing as "love." There is. But sometimes we have to make profound changes of attitude before we can see what love is and make room for love in our lives.

Love betweeen human beings is one of the absolute realities of human nature. Just as soul—Psyche—was one of the gods of the Greek pantheon, so was Love: His name was Eros. For the Greeks understood that love, being an archetype of the collective unconscious, is both eternal and universal in humankind. And for the Greeks, that qualified Love as a god.

Because love is an archetype, it has its own character, its own traits, its own "personality." Like a god, love behaves as a "person" in the unconscious, a separate being in the psyche. Love is distinct from my ego; love was here before my ego came into the world, and love will be here after my ego departs. Yet love is something or "someone" who lives within me. Love is a force that acts from within, that enables my ego to look outside itself, to see my fellow humans as something to be valued and cherished, rather than used.

Therefore, when I say that "I love," it is not I who love, but, in reality, Love who acts through me. Love is not so much something I do as something that I am. Love is not a doing but a state of being—a relatedness, a connectedness to another mortal, an identification with her or him that simply flows within me and through me, independent of my intentions or my efforts.

This state of being may express itself in what I do or in how I treat people, but it can never be reduced to a set of "doings," or acts. It is a feeling within. More often than we realize, love works its divine alchemy best when we follow the advice of Shakespeare's Cordelia: "Love, and keep silent."

Love exists, regardless of our opinions about what it ought to be. No matter how many fabrications or how much selfishness we justify in the name of "love," love still keeps its unchanging character. Its existence and its nature do not depend on my illusions, my opinions, or my counterfeits. Love is different from what my culture has led me to expect, different from what my ego wants, different from the sentimental froth and inflated ecstasies I've been taught to hope for; but love turns out to be real; it turns out to be what I am, rather than what my ego demands.

We need to know this about love. Otherwise we could never stand to look honestly at our self-deceptions. At times people say: "Don't make me see my illusions; if you take away my illusions, there will be nothing left!" We seem to think of love as "man-made," as though we invented it in our minds. Even though romantic love has not turned out to be what we thought, there is still a human love that is inherent in us, and this love will be with us even after our projections, our illusions, and our artifices have all passed away.

Human love is so obscured by the inflations and commotions of romance that we almost never look for love in its own right, and we hardly know what to look for when we do search. But as we learn love's characteristics and attitudes, we can begin to see love within us—revealed in our feelings, in the spontaneous flow of warmth that surges toward another person, in the small, unnoticed acts of relatedness that make up the secret fabric of our daily lives.

Love is the power within us that affirms and values another human being as he or she is. Human love affirms that person who is actually there, rather than the ideal we would like him or her to be or the projection that flows from our minds. Love is the inner god who opens our blind eyes to the beauty, value, and quality of the other person. Love causes us to value that person as a total, individual self, and this means that we accept the negative side as well as the positive, the imperfections as well as the admirable qualities. When one truly loves the human being rather than the projection, one loves the shadow just as one loves the rest. One accepts the other person's totality.

Human love causes a man to see the intrinsic value in a woman; therefore love leads him to honor and serve her, rather than to try to use her for his ego's purposes. When love is guiding him, he is concerned with her needs and her well-being, not fixated on his own wants and whims.

Love alters our sense of importance. Through love we see that the other individual has as great a value in the cosmos as our own; it becomes just as important to us that he or she should be whole, should live fully, should find the joy of life, as that our own needs be met.

In the world of the unconscious, love is one of those great psychological forces that have the power to transform the ego. Love is the one power that awakens the ego to the existence of something outside itself, outside its plans, outside its empire, outside its security. Love relates the ego not only to the rest of the human race, but to the soul and to all the gods of the inner world.

Thus love is by its very nature the exact opposite of egocentricity. We use the word *love* loosely. We use it to dignify any number of demands for attention, power, security, or entertainment from other people. But when we are looking out for our own self-styled "needs," our own desires, our own dreams, and our power over people, this is not love. Love is utterly distinct from our ego's desires and power plays. It leads in a different direction: toward the goodness, the value, and the needs of the people around us.

In its very essence, love is an *appreciation*, a recognition of another's value: It moves a man to honor a woman rather than use her, to ask himself how he might serve her. And if this woman is relating to him through love, she will take the same attitude toward him.

The archetypal nature of love is perhaps nowhere better expressed than in the simple language of Saint Paul:

> Love suffers long and is kind; love does not envy; love does not vaunt itself, is not puffed up. . . . Love does not seek her own way, is not easily provoked, is not anxious to suspect evil . . . bears all things, believes all things, hopes all things, endures all things.
>
> Love never fails: but whether there be prophecies, they shall fail, whether there be tongues, they shall cease, whether there be knowledge, it shall vanish away.

Here is a brief and eloquent statement of the difference between an ego left to its own devices and an ego under the influence of love. My ego is concerned only with itself; but "love suffers long and is kind." My ego is envious, always seeking to inflate itself with illusions of absolute power and control, but "love does not vaunt itself, is not puffed up." My ego, left to its ego-centeredness, will always betray, but "love never fails." My ego only knows how to affirm itself and its desires, but love "seeks not her own way." Love affirms all of life: "bears all things, believes all things, hopes all things."

This is why we have taken exception to romantic love, and this is the main distinction between human love and romantic love: Romance must, by its very nature, deteriorate into egotism. For romance is not a love that is directed at another human being; the passion of romance is always directed at our own projections, our own expectations, our own fantasies. In a very real sense, it is a love not of another person, but of ourselves.

> It should now be clear that to the extent that a relationship is founded on projection the element of human love is lacking. To be in love with someone we do not know as a person, but are attracted to because they reflect back to us the image of the god or goddess in our souls, is, in a sense, to be in love with oneself, not with the other person. In spite of the seeming beauty of the love fantasies we may have in this state of being in love, we can, in fact, be in a thoroughly selfish state of mind.
>
> Real love begins only when one person comes to know another for who he or she really is as a human being, and begins to like and care for that human being.
>
> . . . To be capable of real love means becoming mature, with realistic expectations of the other person. It means accepting responsibility for our own happiness or unhappiness, and neither expecting the other person to make us happy nor blaming that person for our bad moods and frustrations. (Sanford, *Invisible Partners*, pp. 19–20).

When we are focused on our projections, we are

focused on ourselves. And the passion and love we feel for our projections is a reflexive, circular love that is directed inevitably back to ourselves.

But here, again, we run headlong into the paradox of romantic love. The paradox is that we *should* love our projections, and that we should also love ourselves. In romance the love of self becomes distorted; it becomes egocentric and its original nature is lost. But if we learn to seek it on the correct level, the love of self is a true and valid love: It is the second great stream of energy that flows into romantic love, human love's archetypal mate, the other face of Eros.

We need to revere the unconscious parts of ourselves that we project. When we love our projections, when we honor our romantic ideals and fantasies, we affirm infinitely precious dimensions of our total selves. The riddle is how to love one's self without falling into egotism.

As we learn the geography of the human psyche, with its islands of consciousness, its multilayered and multicentered structure, we see that the love of the total self can not be a centering of the universe on our egos. Love of self is the ego's seeking after the other "persons" of the inner world, who hide within us. It is ego's longing for the larger dimensions of the unconscious, its willingness to open itself to the other parts of our total being, and to their points of view, their values, and their needs.

Understood in this way, our love of self is also the "divine" love: our search for the ultimate meaning, for our souls, for the revelation of God. This understanding returns us to the words of Clement of Alexandria:

> Therefore, as it seems, it is the greatest of all disciplines to know oneself; for when a man knows himself, he knows God.

The fault in romantic love is not that we love ourselves, but that we love ourselves wrongly. By trying to revere the unconscious through our romantic projections on other people, we miss the reality hidden in those projections: We don't see that it is our own selves we are searching for.

The task of salvaging love from the swamps of romance begins with a shift of vision toward the inside; we have to wake up to the inner world; we have to learn how to live the "love of self" as an inner experience. But then it is time to redirect our gaze outward again, toward physical people and the relationships we make with them—we must learn the principles of the "human" love.

Many years ago a wise friend gave me a name for human love. She called it "stirring-the-oatmeal" love. She was right: Within this phrase, if we will humble ourselves enough to look, is the very essence of what human love is, and it shows us the principal differences between human love and romance.

Stirring oatmeal is an humble act—not exciting or thrilling. But it symbolizes a relatedness that brings love down to earth. It represents a willingness to share ordinary human life, to find meaning in the simple, unromantic tasks: earning a living, living within a budget, putting out the garbage, feeding the baby in the middle of the night. To "stir the oatmeal" means to find the relatedness, the value, even the beauty, in simple and ordinary things, not to eternally demand a cosmic drama, an entertainment, or an extraordinary intensity in everything. Like the rice hulling of the Zen monks, the spinning wheel of Ghandi, the tent making of Saint Paul, it represents the discovery of the sacred in the midst of the humble and ordinary.

Jung once said that feeling is a matter of the *small.*

And in human love, we can see that it is true. The real relatedness between two people is experienced in the small tasks they do together: the quiet conversation when the day's upheavals are at rest, the soft word of understanding, the daily companionship, the encouragement offered in a difficult moment, the small gift when least expected, the spontaneous gesture of love.

When a couple are genuinely related to each other, they are willing to enter into the whole spectrum of human life together. They transform even the unexciting, difficult, and mundane things into a joyful and fulfilling component of life. By contrast, romantic love can only last so long as a couple are "high" on one another, so long as the money lasts and the entertainments are exciting. "Stirring the oatmeal" means that two people take their love off the airy level of exciting fantasy and convert it into earthy, practical immediacy.

Love is content to do many things that ego is bored with. Love is willing to work with the other person's moods and unreasonableness. Love is willing to fix breakfast and balance the checkbook. Love is willing to do these "oatmeal" things of life because it is related to a person, not a projection.

Human love sees another person as an individual and makes an individualized relationship to him or her. Romantic love sees the other person only as a role player in the drama.

A man's human love desires that a woman become a complete and independent person and encourages her to be herself. Romantic love only affirms what he would like her to be, so that she could be identical to anima. So long as romance rules a man, he affirms a woman only insofar as she is willing to change, so that she may reflect his projected ideal. Romance is never happy with the other person just as he or she is.

Human love necessarily includes friendship: friendship within relationship, within marriage, between husband and wife. When a man and a woman are truly friends, they know each other's difficult points and weaknesses, but they are not inclined to stand in judgment on them. They are more concerned with helping each other and enjoying each other than they are with finding fault.

Friends, genuine friends, are like Kaherdin: They want to affirm rather than to judge; they don't coddle, but neither do they dwell on our inadequacies. Friends back each other up in the tough times, help each other with the sordid and ordinary tasks of life. They don't impose impossible standards on each other, they don't ask for perfection, and they help each other rather than grind each other down with demands.

In romantic love there is no friendship. Romance and friendship are utterly opposed energies, natural enemies with completely opposing motives. Sometimes people say: "I don't want to be friends with my husband [or wife]; it would take all the romance out of our marriage." It is true: Friendship does take the artificial drama and intensity out of a relationship, but it also takes away the egocentricity and the impossibility and replaces the drama with something human and real.

If a man and woman are friends to each other, then they are "neighbors" as well as lovers; their relationship is suddenly subject to Christ's dictum: "Love thy neighbor as thyself." One of the glaring contradictions in romantic love is that so many couples treat their friends with so much more kindness, consideration, generosity, and forgiveness than they ever give to one another! When people are with their friends, they are charming, helpful, and courteous. But when they come home, they often vent all their anger, resentments, moods, and frustrations on each other. Strangely, they treat their friends better than they do each other.

When two people are "in love," people commonly say that they are "more than just friends." But in the long run, they seem to treat each other as *less* than friends. Most people think that being "in love" is a much more intimate, much more "meaningful," relationship than "mere" friendship. Why, then, do couples refuse each other the selfless love, the kindness and good will, that they readily give to their friends? People can't ask of their friends that they carry all their projections, be scapegoats for all their moods, keep them feeling happy, and make life complete for them. Why do couples impose these demands on each other? Because the cult of romance teaches us that we have the right to expect that all our projections will be borne—all our desires satisfied, and all our fantasies made to come true—in the person we are "in love" with. In one of the Hindu rites of marriage, the bride and groom make to each other a solemn statement: "You will be my *best friend.*" Western couples need to learn to be friends, to live with each other in a spirit of friendship, to take the quality of friendship as a guide through the tangles we have made of love.

We can learn much of human love by learning to look with an open mind at Oriental cultures and their attitudes.

During the time I spent in India and Japan, I saw marriages and love relationships that are not based at all on romance but on a warm, devoted, and enduring love. Hindus are instinctive masters of the art of human love. I think this is because they have never taken on romantic love as a way of trying to relate to each other. Hindus automatically make the differentiation that we have completely muddled in the West: They know how to worship anima, the archetypes, the gods, as inner realities; they know how to keep their experience of the divine side of life distinct from their personal relationships and marriages.

Hindus take the inner world on a symbolic level; they translate the inner archetypes into images and external symbols through temple art and allegorical ritual. But they don't project the inner gods onto their husbands and wives. They take the personified archetypes as symbols of another world and take each other as human beings; as a result, they don't put impossible demands on each other and they don't disappoint each other.

A Hindu man does not ask of his wife that she be anima or that she take him off to another world or that she embody all the intensity and perfection of his inner life. Since lyrical religious experience is still part of their culture, Hindus do not try to make their marriages and human relationships into a substitute for communion with the soul. They find their gods in the temple, in meditation, or sometimes in the guru; they don't try to make the outer relationship serve the role of the inner one.

At first a Westerner is confused by the Hindu way; their love doesn't seem to be bubbling with enough heat and intensity to suit the Western romantic taste. But if one observes patiently, one is startled out of Western prejudices and begins to question the assumption that romance is the only "true love." There is a quiet but steady lovingness in Hindu marriages, a profound affection. There is stability: They are not caught in the dramatic oscillations between "in love" and "out of love," adoration and disillusionment, that Western couples are.

In the traditional Hindu marriage, a man's commitment to his wife does not depend on his staying "in love" with her. Since he was never "in love" in the first place, there is no way he can fall "out of love." His relationship to his wife is based on loving *her,* not on being "in love" with an ideal that he projects onto her. His relationship is not going to collapse because one day he falls "out of love," or because he meets another woman who catches his projection. He is committed to a woman and a family, not to a projection.

We think of ourselves as more sophisticated than the "simple" Hindus. But, by comparison with a Hindu, the average Western man is like an ox with a ring in his nose, following his projection around from one woman to another, making no true relationship or commitment to any. In the area of human feeling, love, and relationship, Hindus have evolved a highly differentiated, subtle, and refined consciousness. In these matters, they do better than we.

One of the most striking and surprising things I observed among traditional Hindus was how bright, happy, and psychologically healthy their children are. Children in Hindu families are not neurotic; they are not torn within themselves as so many Western children are. They are bathed constantly in human affection, and they sense a peaceful flow of affection between their mother and father. They sense the stability. the enduring quality of their family life. Their parents are committed permanently; they don't hear their parents asking themselves whether their marriage is "going to work out"; separation and divorce do not float as specters in the air.

For us Westerners there is no turning back of the clock. We can't go the way of the Hindus; we can't solve our Western dilemma by doing an imitation of other people's customs or other people's attitudes. We can't pretend that we have an Eastern psyche rather than a Western psyche. We have to deal with our own Western unconscious and our own Western wounds; we have to find the healing balm within our own Western soul. We have drunk the love potion and plunged into the romantic era of our evolution, and the only way out is by the path that leads straight ahead. We can't go back, and we may not linger.

But we can learn from the Eastern cultures to stand outside ourselves, outside our assumptions and our beliefs, just long enough to see ourselves in a new perspective. We can learn what it is to approach love with a different set of attitudes, unburdened by the dogmas of our culture.

We can learn that human relationship is inseparable from friendship and commitment. We can learn that the essence of love is not to use the other to make us happy but to serve and affirm the one we love. And we can discover, to our surprise, that what we have needed more than anything was not so much to be loved, as to love.

Bibliography

Publications Quoted in the Text

de Rougemont, Denis. *Love in the Western World.* Translated by Montgomery Belgion. New York: Pantheon Books, 1956.

Hillman, James. "Anima." *Spring* 1973.

______. "Anima (II)." *Spring* 1974.

______. *Revisioning Psychology.* New York: Harper & Row, Harper Colophon, 1977.

The I Ching. Translated from Chinese to German by Richard Wilhelm and rendered into English by Cary F. Baynes, with a foreword by C. G. Jung. Bollingen Series XIX. Princeton: Princeton University Press, 1967.

Jung, Carl G. *Aion.* Translated by R. F. C. Hull. 9 C.W., part 2. Bollingen Series XX. Princeton: Princeton University Press, 1959.

______. "Psychological Commentary on Kundalini Yoga." *Spring* 1975 and 1976.

______. *The Psychology of the Transference.* 16 C.W. Bollingen Series XX. Princeton: Princeton University Press, 1966.

Neihardt, John G. *Black Elk Speaks.* New York: William Morrow, 1932; New York: Simon & Schuster, Pocket Book, 1972.

Sanford, John A. *The Invisible Partners.* New York: Paulist Press, 1980.

Sources of, and Commentary on, the Myth

Bédier, Joseph. *The Romance of Tristan as Retold by Joseph Bédier.* Translated by Hillaire Belloc and Paul Rosenfeld. New York: Vintage Books, 1945; New York: Doubleday, Anchor Books, 1965.

Béroul. *The Romance of Tristan* and *Tristan's Madness (La Folie Tristan).* Translated by Alan S. Fedrick. Harmondsworth: Penguin Books, 1970.

de Rougemont, Denis. *Love Declared: Essays on the Myths of Love.* Translated by Richard Howard. New York: Pantheon Books, 1963.

______. *Love in the Western World.* Translated by Montgomery Belgion. New York: Pantheon Books, 1956.

Gottfried von Strassburg. *Tristan, with Surviving Fragments of Thomas of England.* Translated by A. T. Hatto. Baltimore: Penguin Books, 1960.

Loomis, Gertrude, and Loomis, Roger Sherman. *Tristan and Iseult: A Study of the Sources of the Romance.* 2d ed. New York: Burt Franklin, 1960.

Thomas of Britain. *The Romance of Tristam & Ysolt.* Translated from Old French and Old Norse by Roger Sherman Loomis. New York: Columbia University Press, 1951.

Other Related Works

Campbell, Joseph. *Myths to Live By.* New York: Viking Press, 1972.

______. *The Portable Jung.* New York: Viking Press, 1972.

de Castillejo, Irene C. *Knowing Woman.* New York: G. P. Putnam's Sons, 1973.

Johnson, Robert A. *He: Understanding Masculine Psychology.* King of Prussia, Pa.: Religious Publishing, 1974; New York: Harper & Row Perennial Library, 1977.

______. *She: Understanding Feminine Psychology.* King of Prussia, Pa.: Religious Publishing, 1976; New York: Harper & Row Perennial Library, 1977.

Jung, Carl Gustav. *Man and His Symbols.* Garden City, N.Y.: Doubleday, 1964.

———. *Archetypes of the Collective Unconscious.* 9 C.W., part 1. New York: Pantheon Books, 1959.

———. *Memories, Dreams and Reflections.* New York: Pantheon Books, 1963.

Jung, Emma, and Von Franz, Marie-Louise. *The Grail Legend.* A C. G. Jung Foundation Book. New York: G. P. Putnam's Sons, 1970.

Neumann, Erich. *Amor and Psyche.* New York: Pantheon Books, 1956.

Sanford, John A. *The Kingdom Within.* New York: J. B. Lippincott, 1970.

Von Franz, Marie-Louise. *The Problem of the Feminine in Fairy Tales.* New York & Zurich: Spring Publications, 1972.

Whitmont, Edward C. *The Symbolic Quest.* New York: G. P. Putnam's Sons, 1969; New York: Harper & Row, 1973.

Helen of Troy